HOPE, HEALING AND RISING STRONG: A SERIES ON DOMESTIC VIOLENCE

FINDING YOUR VOICE: OVERCOMING VERBAL ABUSE

Trient Press
3375 S Rainbow Blvd
#81710, SMB 13135
Las Vegas,NV 89180

Ordering Information:
Quantity sales. Special discounts are available on quantity purchases by corporations, associations, and others. For details, contact the publisher at the address above.
Orders by U.S. trade bookstores and wholesalers. Please contact Trient Press: Tel: (775) 996-3844; or visit www.trientpress.com.

Printed in the United States of America

Publisher's Cataloging-in-Publication data
Ruscsak, M.L.
A title of a book :Working for Your Dreams: Making this year your best year
ISBN
Paperback   978-1-955198-86-8
E-book   978-1-955198-87-5

PART 1
INTRODUCTION

Overview of the series "Hope, Healing and Rising Strong"

Welcome to the third installment of the "Hope, Healing and Rising Strong" series. This series is dedicated to inspiring and empowering individuals who have been through traumatic experiences and are now on a journey to reclaim their power, find their voice and rise strong.

Explanation of the theme of this third book "Finding Your Voice: Overcoming Verbal Abuse"

In this book, we delve into the damaging effects of verbal abuse and the importance of finding your voice. Verbal abuse is a type of emotional abuse that can leave deep scars and shatter self-esteem. But it's never too late to heal and find your voice. Through this book, you will learn about the healing process and discover the power of your voice.

Brief overview of the purpose of the book and the target audience

The purpose of this book is to provide support, guidance, and inspiration to individuals who have experienced verbal abuse. This book is for anyone who has felt unheard, invalidated, or manipulated through words. Whether you're just starting your journey to healing or looking to strengthen your voice, this book is for you.

Explanation of why the topic of verbal abuse is important

Verbal abuse is a pervasive issue that affects millions of people, but it is often overlooked and minimized. The impact of verbal abuse can be just as damaging as physical abuse, yet it can be harder to recognize and overcome. By speaking out and sharing our experiences, we can raise awareness and help others on their journey to healing. Together, we can break the cycle of abuse and reclaim our power.

CHAPTER 1: OVERVIEW OF THE SERIES "HOPE, HEALING AND RISING STRONG"

As a survivor of abuse, I understand the pain and struggle that comes with the journey towards healing. But I also know that with the right support and guidance, it is possible to overcome the obstacles and rise strong. That is why I am so proud to be a part of the "Hope, Healing and Rising Strong" series, a powerful and transformative collection of books that offer hope and inspiration to survivors of different types of abuse.

The first book in the series, "Rising Strong: A Survivor's Guide to Thriving After Domestic Violence," is a testament to the resilience of the human spirit and a source of empowerment for those who have suffered from domestic violence. Through personal stories, expert advice, and practical exercises, this book guides survivors on their journey to recovery, providing them with the tools and support they need to heal and rise above their experiences. Whether you're just starting your journey of recovery or you're well on your way, "Rising Strong" will provide you with the encouragement, guidance, and inspiration you need to heal and thrive.

The second book, "Embracing Empowerment: Overcoming Psychological Abuse," is for anyone who has experienced the devastating effects of psychological abuse. This book offers a roadmap for reclaiming your life and finding happiness and peace, filled with practical tips, techniques, and guidance from survivors who have successfully navigated the journey to healing and empowerment. From facing and processing the trauma, to re-establishing safety and security, to building a positive self-image, this book provides the tools, resources, and support needed to overcome psychological abuse and create a brighter, more fulfilling future.

With this third book, "Finding Your Voice: Overcoming Verbal Abuse," we delve into the damaging effects of verbal abuse and the importance of finding your voice. This book offers support, guidance, and inspiration to individuals who have experienced verbal abuse, providing them with the tools and resources they need to heal and reclaim their power.

Together, the "Hope, Healing and Rising Strong" series serves as a powerful reminder that no matter what you've been through, you have the strength to rise above it and create a better future for yourself and those around you. So, let's begin this journey of healing, growth, and empowerment, and embrace the power within us to rise strong.

CHAPTER 2: EXPLANATION OF THE THEME OF "FINDING YOUR VOICE: OVERCOMING VERBAL ABUSE"

Verbal abuse can be a silent and insidious form of abuse, yet it can have a profound impact on one's mental and emotional well-being. The words we hear, whether spoken by loved ones, friends, or coworkers, can shape our self-image, our self-esteem, and our outlook on life. Verbal abuse can leave deep wounds that may not be visible to others, but that can last a lifetime.

As a survivor of verbal abuse, I know the pain and struggle that comes with trying to find your voice and reclaim your power. I remember feeling trapped and powerless, like my voice didn't matter and that I didn't have the right to speak up for myself. But I also remember the moment when I found the courage to speak up, to reclaim my voice, and to take back control of my life.

In "Finding Your Voice: Overcoming Verbal Abuse," we explore the many facets of verbal abuse and the ways in which it can affect our lives. We delve into the psychological impact of verbal abuse and the ways in which it can impact our self-esteem and self-worth. We also explore the importance of speaking up and reclaiming our voice, as well as the steps we can take to heal and move forward.

Through personal stories, expert advice, and practical exercises, this book offers hope and inspiration to individuals who have experienced verbal abuse. Whether you're just beginning your journey of healing or you're well on your way, "Finding Your Voice" provides you with the support, guidance, and resources you need to reclaim your power and find your voice.

In this book, we explore the various forms of verbal abuse, from name-calling and belittling to gaslighting and manipulation. We also discuss the importance of setting healthy boundaries, of learning to communicate effectively, and of seeking support from friends, family, and professionals.

This book is not only a guide to overcoming verbal abuse, but also a call to action. It is a reminder that your voice matters, that your experiences are valid, and that you have the strength to reclaim your power and rise above the challenges of verbal abuse. So, let us begin this journey together, and find the courage to reclaim our voices, heal, and rise strong.

Survivor's Story:

My name is Nicole, and I'm a survivor of verbal abuse. My journey began in middle school, when I started to feel like I didn't fit in. I was always the quiet one, the one who preferred to keep to herself and stay out of the spotlight. But then, I started to hear the whispers and the taunts from my classmates. They called me names, made fun of my clothes, and belittled me in front of others.

At first, I tried to ignore it. I told myself that they didn't really mean it, that it was just a joke. But the more they taunted me, the more I started to believe that there was something wrong with me. I felt like I was trapped in a cycle of negative thoughts and self-doubt, and I couldn't seem to escape.

It wasn't until I started seeing a therapist that I realized what was happening to me. She helped me understand that I was experiencing verbal abuse, and that it was taking a toll on my mental and emotional well-being. With her support, I started to see myself in a different light. I started to understand that the things my classmates were saying weren't true, and that I was a strong, capable young woman with so much to offer.

With the help of my therapist, I also started to find my voice. I learned to stand up for myself and to set boundaries with those who were hurting me. I practiced speaking up in safe spaces, and gradually started to feel more confident and empowered.

Now, as a high school student, I'm proud to say that I have found my voice. I no longer let the taunts and belittling of my classmates get to me. I have a strong support system, and I know that I have the strength and resilience to rise above the challenges of verbal abuse.

I hope that by sharing my story, I can inspire others to find their voice and reclaim their power. No matter what you've been through, no matter how alone or powerless you may feel, know that you are not alone. You have the strength to heal, to rise above the challenges, and to find the happiness and peace you deserve.

Journal Exercises

Here are some journal exercises that can help you process your experiences with verbal abuse and start finding your voice:

Reflection: Take some time to reflect on your experiences with verbal abuse. Write about what you remember feeling and thinking at the time.

_____

_____

_____

_____

_____

_____

_____

_____

_____

_____

_____

What were some of the negative thoughts and beliefs
that you had about yourself as a result of the abuse?

_____

_____

_____

_____

_____

_____

_____

_____

_____

_____

How have these thoughts and beliefs affected your life?

_____

_____

_____

_____

_____

_____

_____

_____

_____

_____

Self-Affirmations: Write down 10 positive affirmations about yourself. These can be things like "I am strong," "I am deserving of love and respect," or "I am capable of overcoming any challenge." Read these affirmations every day and remind yourself of your strengths and worth.

_____

_____

_____

_____

_____

_____

_____

_____

_____

Boundary-Setting: Think about the people in your life who have contributed to your experiences with verbal abuse. How do you want to set boundaries with these individuals moving forward?

_____

_____

_____

_____

_____

_____

_____

_____

Write down a plan for setting these boundaries, including what you want to say and how you want to communicate.

_____

_____

_____

_____

_____

_____

_____

_____

_____

Gratitude: Take some time to think about all the things you are grateful for in your life. Write down a list of 10 things that bring you joy and happiness. Reflect on these things and allow yourself to feel a sense of gratitude and peace.

_____

_____

_____

_____

_____

_____

_____

Empowered Self-Talk: Write down some of the negative self-talk that you have been experiencing as a result of verbal abuse. Then, rewrite these thoughts in a more empowering and positive way. For example, instead of thinking "I'm not good enough," try thinking "I am good enough, just as I am." Repeat these empowering self-talk statements to yourself throughout the day.

Remember, these exercises are just a starting point. You can continue to reflect and grow in any way that feels meaningful and empowering to you. The most important thing is to be kind and gentle with yourself, and to recognize your own strengths and resilience.

CHAPTER 3: BRIEF OVERVIEW OF THE PURPOSE OF THE BOOK AND THE TARGET AUDIENCE

The purpose of "Finding Your Voice: Overcoming Verbal Abuse" is to empower and inspire survivors of verbal abuse to reclaim their voice and find healing. This book is for anyone who has experienced the harmful effects of verbal abuse and is seeking to overcome the trauma, build their self-esteem, and create a better future.

Whether you're still in the early stages of recovery or you're well on your way, this book is designed to provide you with the tools, resources, and support you need to find your voice and move forward with hope and empowerment. We understand that every survivor's journey is unique, and that's why this book is written in a way that allows you to customize your journey to your specific needs and experiences.

The target audience for this book is anyone who has experienced verbal abuse, including but not limited to:

Teens who have been bullied or tormented by their classmates

Adults who have experienced emotional or psychological abuse from partners or family members.

Survivors of domestic violence who have experienced verbal abuse as part of their trauma.

This book is also for those who are seeking to support and empower a loved one who has experienced verbal abuse. Whether you're a parent, a partner, a friend, or a family member, this book will provide you with the knowledge and tools you need to support and encourage your loved one on their journey to healing and empowerment.

In this book, you'll learn about the different forms of verbal abuse, and how to recognize the warning signs. You'll also discover practical strategies for overcoming the effects of verbal abuse, and rebuilding your self-esteem and confidence. Whether you're struggling with feelings of fear, shame, or anger, you'll find guidance and support in these pages.

Most importantly, this book is a celebration of the resilience and strength of survivors everywhere. It's a testament to the power of the human spirit to overcome adversity, and a reminder that no matter what you've been through, you have the courage and the determination to rise above it and find happiness and fulfillment.

So, if you're ready to reclaim your voice and start your journey to healing and empowerment, we invite you to open this book and begin your journey today. Together, we will find the strength, courage, and hope to overcome verbal abuse and create a better future for ourselves and those around us.

A Parent's Story

Hello Dear Reader,

This letter is a parent's warning, a testament to the devastating effects of verbal abuse and bullying. As someone who has been affected by these experiences, both as a victim and now as a parent, I feel a deep sense of urgency to share my story and encourage others to take this issue seriously. It is my hope that by speaking out and sharing my journey, I can help others understand the importance of addressing verbal abuse and bullying, and provide them with the tools and support they need to protect themselves and those they love.

I never could have imagined the pain and heartbreak of losing my child to verbal abuse. Looking back now, I can see the warning signs – the changes in my child's behavior, the way they seemed to withdraw from the world, the way they talked about feeling hopeless and helpless. But at the time, I didn't understand the gravity of what was happening.

I thought my child was just going through the normal ups and downs of high school, that the teasing and name-calling was just a part of growing up. But now I know that verbal abuse is a serious issue that can have devastating effects on a person's mental and emotional health.

As a parent, it's easy to feel helpless in the face of something like this. We want to protect our children from harm, but it's not always clear what we can do to help. And now, with the added power of the internet and social media, bullying has evolved in ways that I never could have imagined.

If only I had known about books like "Finding Your Voice: Overcoming Verbal Abuse" 10 years ago. Maybe things would have turned out differently for my child. Maybe they would still be here with us today.

But even though it's too late for my child, I know that I can still help others. I can share my story and raise awareness about the importance of recognizing and addressing verbal abuse. And by sharing the tools and resources in this book, I can help others find the support they need to overcome the effects of bullying and find their own path to healing.

As someone who was bullied in school myself, I understand the feelings of fear and isolation that come with being a target of abuse. But I also know that there is hope, and that it's possible to overcome these experiences and find the strength and resilience to rise above it all.

So, to anyone out there who is struggling with verbal abuse, or who has a loved one who is, I want you to know that you're not alone. And to anyone who has suffered the loss of a child to bullying, I want to extend my deepest condolences. Together, let's raise awareness about the dangers of verbal abuse and help those in need find their voice and start their journey to healing and empowerment.

As I close this letter, my heart is heavy with the memory of my child, who I will always love and miss deeply. But I also feel a sense of purpose and determination, to do all I can to help prevent others from experiencing the same tragedy that we have. By sharing my story, I hope to raise awareness about the dangers of verbal abuse, and encourage others to take it seriously and seek help when needed.

To anyone reading this who may be struggling with verbal abuse, I want you to know that you are not alone, and that there is hope. You have the strength and resilience to overcome this, and you deserve to live a life free from fear, pain, and hurt.

So, I end this letter with a message of hope, for those who have suffered from verbal abuse, and for their families. I hope that this book, "Finding Your Voice: Overcoming Verbal Abuse," will be a source of support, encouragement, and empowerment, as you begin your journey to recovery and healing. Together, we can make a difference, and help create a world where verbal abuse is not tolerated, and where all people can live with dignity, respect, and joy.

Journal Exercises

Reflection: Take a moment to reflect on your own experiences with verbal abuse. Write down any memories or emotions that come to mind.

_____

_____

_____

_____

_____

_____

_____

_____

_____

Empowerment: Write a letter to yourself, offering words of encouragement and empowerment. Remind yourself of your strength and resilience, and affirm your ability to overcome the effects of verbal abuse.

_____

_____

_____

_____

_____

_____

_____

_____

_____

_____

_____

_____

_____

_____

_____

_____

_____

_____

Gratitude: Write a list of things you are grateful for, including the people in your life who have offered support and encouragement. Focus on the positive aspects of your life, and let gratitude guide your thoughts and feelings.

_____

_____

_____

_____

_____

_____

_____

_____

_____

Boundaries: Write about the importance of setting and maintaining healthy boundaries, both for yourself and for others. Think about what boundaries you need to set in your own life, and what steps you can take to ensure that your boundaries are respected.

_____

_____

_____

_____

_____

_____

_____

_____

_____

_____

Support: Write about the importance of seeking support from others, and the role that friends, family, and professionals can play in helping you overcome the effects of verbal abuse. Reflect on your own experiences with seeking support, and identify any challenges or obstacles that you may need to overcome in order to access the support you need.

_____

_____

_____

_____

_____

_____

_____

_____

_____

_____

_____

_____

_____

_____

_____

_____

_____

_____

_____

_____

_____

_____

_____

_____

_____

_____

_____

_____

_____

_____

Coping Strategies: Write about the different coping strategies you have used in the past to manage the effects of verbal abuse. Consider what has worked well for you, and what has not, and make a plan for how you can continue to build resilience and find effective coping strategies in the future.

CHAPTER 4: EXPLANATION OF WHY THE TOPIC OF VERBAL ABUSE IS IMPORTANT

Verbal abuse is a silent killer, one that often goes unnoticed and unrecognized by those around us. It is a form of violence that can be just as damaging, if not more so, than physical abuse. Verbal abuse is insidious, creeping into our lives and eroding our self-esteem, our confidence, and our sense of self. It leaves deep scars, both physically and emotionally, and can impact us for the rest of our lives.

That's why it's so important that we talk about verbal abuse, and why it is the focus of this third book in the Hope, Healing and Rising Strong series. This book is a call to action, a powerful reminder that no matter what you've been through, you have the strength to rise above it and create a better future for yourself and those around you. It's a message of hope and empowerment, reminding us all that we have the power to change our lives, to heal from our experiences, and to find our voice.

But why is the topic of verbal abuse so important? For starters, it's an all-too-common experience. Nearly everyone has been affected by verbal abuse in some way, whether it's in their personal relationships, in their workplace, or even in school. The impact of verbal abuse can be devastating, affecting everything from our mental and physical health to our relationships and career.

Furthermore, verbal abuse often goes unnoticed and unrecognized, meaning that the victims are often left feeling isolated, helpless, and hopeless. They may feel like they're the only one going through this, that nobody will believe them or understand what they're going through. This can lead to feelings of shame, self-blame, and low self-esteem.

That's why it's so important that we bring the topic of verbal abuse out into the open, and start having conversations about it. By doing so, we can help to reduce the stigma and shame surrounding verbal abuse, and provide a safe and supportive space for those who have experienced it to heal and find their voice. This book is a step in that direction, offering practical tools and guidance to help you overcome the effects of verbal abuse and reclaim your life.

So, whether you're a survivor of verbal abuse, or a loved one seeking to support someone who has been affected, this book is for you. It's a reminder that you're not alone, that there's hope, and that you have the strength to rise above the challenges of verbal abuse and create a better future for yourself and those around you.

A survivor's story

Dear reader,

I want to share my story with you, a story of hope and perseverance. A story about overcoming verbal abuse and bullying, and rising above it all. My name is John and I am a survivor of bullying and verbal abuse that started in middle school and continued through high school.

Growing up, I was an easy target for bullies. I was small for my age and didn't fit in with the popular crowd. I was often called names, teased, and made to feel like an outcast. This continued into high school, and the bullying only got worse. The constant insults and harassment began to take a toll on me. I felt like I was worthless and that no one cared about me. I even thought about taking my own life at one point.

It wasn't until my parents intervened that I started to get help. They took me to see a therapist, and with their support, I began to work through my experiences of bullying and verbal abuse. I learned that what had happened to me wasn't my fault, and that I was deserving of love and respect. I also learned coping skills and ways to protect myself from further harm.

Years later, I'm proud to say that I am a changed person. I have graduated high school and am on the verge of graduating from college. I have found my voice and have become an advocate for those who are still struggling with bullying and verbal abuse. I want to show others that there is hope, and that it is possible to rise above the pain and find happiness and fulfillment.

My story is just one of many, but I hope it will serve as a source of inspiration for those who are going through similar struggles. You are not alone, and there is help available. You too can rise above the pain and find the light in the darkness.

Sincerely,
John

Journal Exercises

Write down the key moments in your life when you experienced verbal abuse and how it affected you. Reflect on how you felt during those moments and what you wish you had known or done differently.

Identify a person or a group of people who have been a source of support for you in overcoming verbal abuse. Write a letter to them expressing your gratitude and what their support meant to you.

Imagine yourself as the person you want to be, free from the effects of verbal abuse. Write down what you would do differently, how you would react to situations, and what your life would look like.

Create a personal mantra or affirmations that you can repeat to yourself when you are feeling triggered by verbal abuse. Write them down and place them somewhere you will see them often as a reminder of your strength and resilience.

Write a letter to your younger self, offering advice and encouragement on how to cope with verbal abuse. Think about what you would have wanted to hear and what would have made a difference for you at that time.

Identify one small step you can take to start reclaiming your voice and power after experiencing verbal abuse. Write down what it is and how it will help you on your journey of healing and growth.

Reflect on the impact that verbal abuse has had on your relationships, your self-esteem, and your overall well-being. Write down what you want to work on in order to heal and improve these areas of your life.

PART 2
UNDERSTANDING
VERBAL ABUSE

In Part 2 of our book, "Finding Your Voice: Overcoming Verbal Abuse," we dive deeper into the topic of verbal abuse, exploring its definition, characteristics, and impacts on individuals. Through this section, we aim to provide a better understanding of what verbal abuse is and how it can affect a person's life.

We'll explore the different forms of verbal abuse and the impact it can have on a person's self-esteem, confidence, and mental health. We'll also delve into the reasons why people engage in verbal abuse, and what can be done to prevent it from happening.

By the end of Part 2, readers will have a comprehensive understanding of verbal abuse, and the ways in which it can affect a person's life. This knowledge will serve as a foundation for the practical tools and strategies provided in Part 3, where we'll focus on empowering survivors to overcome verbal abuse and reclaim their voices.

CHAPTER 5: DEFINITION OF VERBAL ABUSE

Verbal abuse is a form of psychological abuse that involves the use of words and language to demean, control, manipulate, or harm someone. Verbal abuse is not limited to physical violence or overt aggression, but can involve a wide range of behaviors that are intended to harm someone emotionally or psychologically. This type of abuse can take many forms, including name-calling, mocking, belittling, threatening, or even ignoring someone. The harm caused by verbal abuse can be just as severe as the harm caused by physical abuse and can have lasting effects on a person's self-esteem, mental health, and overall well-being.

Verbal abuse can be difficult to recognize and can often be dismissed as harmless teasing or just a difference in communication styles. However, it is important to understand that verbal abuse is never okay and can have devastating effects on those who experience it. Verbal abuse can take many different forms, including shouting, sarcasm, bullying, humiliation, and insults. It can be used to control or manipulate someone, or to undermine their confidence and self-esteem. Verbal abuse can also involve the use of passive-aggressive behavior, such as ignoring someone or giving them the silent treatment, which can be just as damaging as overt aggression.

The effects of verbal abuse can be long-lasting and far-reaching, affecting a person's self-esteem, mental health, and overall well-being. Verbal abuse can cause a person to feel ashamed, humiliated, and worthless, leading to feelings of anxiety, depression, and low self-worth. It can also cause a person to question their own reality, leading to feelings of confusion and self-doubt. The impact of verbal abuse can be especially devastating for children and teenagers, who are still in the process of developing their sense of self and self-worth.

In conclusion, it is important to understand the definition of verbal abuse and recognize its harmful effects. It is never okay for someone to use their words to harm or control another person, and it is crucial to seek help and support if you or someone you know is experiencing verbal abuse. The next chapters of this book will explore the various characteristics of verbal abuse and its impact on individuals, as well as the reasons behind why people engage in verbal abuse. Through a better understanding of verbal abuse, we can empower those who have experienced it and help them find their voice and reclaim their lives.

Survivor's Story

As a therapist with over two decades of experience, I have seen the devastating impact of verbal abuse on countless individuals. I have walked alongside survivors on their journey to healing and watched as they have found their voice and reclaimed their power. But despite the progress we have made in raising awareness about the harms of verbal abuse, it remains a pervasive issue that continues to affect people from all walks of life.

Verbal abuse can take many forms, from cruel and hurtful words to subtle and insidious forms of degradation and control. It can come from partners, friends, family members, or even strangers. Regardless of its source, verbal abuse is a serious issue that can have a profound impact on the mental, emotional, and physical well-being of those who experience it.

Despite the devastating impact of verbal abuse, I have also seen the resilience and strength of the human spirit. I have witnessed survivors who have overcome incredible odds to heal, grow, and thrive. And it is with this hope and inspiration that I write this message of hope.

To anyone who is currently experiencing verbal abuse, or has experienced it in the past, know that you are not alone. You are not to blame for the hurtful words and actions of others, and you have the power to overcome them. With the help of supportive professionals and a strong community of allies, you can find your voice, reclaim your power, and rise above the abuse.

So, whether you are just starting your journey of healing, or are further along the path, know that you have the strength and resilience to rise above the abuse and create a better future for yourself. And remember, no matter how dark the days may seem, there is always hope and the possibility of healing and growth.

Journal exercises

Reflecting on the definition: Write down your own understanding of what verbal abuse is, and then compare it to the definition provided in this chapter. Consider the ways in which your definition may have evolved over time, and what has led you to this point.

Personal experiences: Write about a time when you experienced verbal abuse. Reflect on how you felt during and after the incident, and how it impacted you. Think about the ways in which verbal abuse has affected your life and relationships, and what you have learned from these experiences.

_____

_____

_____

_____

_____

_____

_____

_____

_____

Understanding the effects: Take some time to consider the impact of verbal abuse on different individuals and communities. Reflect on the ways in which verbal abuse can harm mental and emotional health, and how it can impact self-esteem and confidence.

_____

_____

_____

_____

_____

_____

_____

_____

_____

_____

Taking action: Think about what you can do to help those who have experienced verbal abuse. Write down specific steps you can take, such as volunteering, donating, or advocating for policy change.

_____

_____

_____

_____

_____

_____

_____

_____

_____

_____

_____

Reflections on the future: Consider what you would like to see change in regards to verbal abuse in the future. Write about your hopes, dreams, and aspirations for a world free from this form of harm.

CHAPTER 6: CHARACTERISTICS OF VERBAL ABUSE AND ITS IMPACT ON INDIVIDUALS

Verbal abuse can take many forms and can be difficult to recognize, especially when it is subtle or disguised as jokes or teasing. However, it is important to be aware of the common characteristics of verbal abuse so that we can identify it and seek help when necessary. In this chapter, we will explore the different forms that verbal abuse can take, and how it can impact individuals in a negative way.

One of the most common forms of verbal abuse is name-calling. This can involve using hurtful or demeaning words to describe someone, and can be directed at their appearance, character, or abilities. This type of verbal abuse can be especially damaging because it can chip away at a person's self-esteem and confidence over time.

Another characteristic of verbal abuse is constant criticism. This can take the form of a barrage of negative comments, whether they are directed at a person's performance, their choices, or their overall character. This type of abuse can be especially devastating because it can leave the victim feeling like they can never do anything right, and can erode their confidence in themselves.

Verbal abuse can also involve controlling and manipulative behavior. This can involve a person using threats, intimidation, or ultimatums to control their victim. This type of abuse can have a significant impact on a person's mental health, as it can leave them feeling trapped, helpless, and unable to make decisions for themselves.

Verbal abuse can also involve gaslighting, which is when a person manipulates the victim into doubting their own perceptions or memories. This can be incredibly confusing and disorienting for the victim, as they may begin to question their own sanity.

The impact of verbal abuse on individuals can be far-reaching and long-lasting. It can damage a person's self-esteem, confidence, and mental health, leaving them feeling anxious, depressed, and hopeless. It can also affect their relationships with others, as they may struggle to trust people and form close connections.

In conclusion, recognizing and understanding the characteristics of verbal abuse and its impact on individuals is crucial in addressing and overcoming it. Verbal abuse can have devastating effects on a person's self-esteem, confidence, and mental health, and is often underestimated or overlooked. It is important for individuals who have experienced verbal abuse to seek support and work towards healing and recovery, and for society to be more aware of the issue and make efforts to prevent it. The journey towards healing and recovery can be challenging, but with the right resources and support, individuals affected by verbal abuse can reclaim their power and voice.

A Survivor's Story

My name is Jessica, and I come from a loving family where negative words were never used to harm someone. Growing up, I never thought I would ever experience verbal abuse, let alone become a victim of it. But that all changed when I got married to my first husband.

At first, he was charming, attentive, and caring. But as time went on, I started to notice a shift in his behavior. He would criticize me for small things, like the way I dressed or the way I cooked dinner. At first, I brushed it off and thought it was just his way of offering constructive criticism. But as time went on, the criticism became more frequent and more damaging.

He would use words to break me down little by little, chipping away at my self-esteem and confidence. I started to believe that I was worthless and that I would never be good enough. I felt trapped in the relationship, unsure of how to get out or who to turn to for help.

It wasn't until a close friend of mine confronted me about the situation that I realized what was happening to me. She helped me understand that I was a victim of verbal abuse and that I needed to get out of the relationship and seek help.

With the support of my family, friends, and professionals, I was able to leave my husband and start the journey towards healing and recovery. It was a long and difficult road, but with the right resources and support, I was able to reclaim my power and find my voice again.

Now, years later, I am a strong and confident woman. I have dedicated my life to helping others who have experienced verbal abuse, and I want to share a message of hope with all those who are still struggling. No matter how dark it may seem, there is always a way forward, and you are never alone.

Journal Exercises

Reflect on your own experiences with verbal abuse. What are some of the characteristics of verbal abuse that you have experienced or observed?

_____

_____

_____

_____

_____

_____

_____

_____

_____

_____

Think about the impact that verbal abuse has had on you or someone you know. How has it affected self-esteem, confidence, and mental health?

_____

_____

_____

_____

_____

_____

_____

_____

_____

Write a letter to yourself from the perspective of your future self, in which you offer words of encouragement and hope for overcoming the effects of verbal abuse.

_____

_____

_____

_____

_____

_____

_____

_____

_____

Create a list of self-care activities and techniques that you can use to boost your self-esteem and mental well-being, such as meditation, exercise, journaling, or spending time in nature.

_____

_____

_____

_____

_____

_____

_____

_____

_____

_____

Write about a time when you stood up for yourself or someone else against verbal abuse. Reflect on the feelings and thoughts that you experienced, and how you were able to overcome them.

_____

_____

_____

_____

_____

_____

_____

_____

_____

_____

Make a collage or a mind map that represents your journey towards healing and recovery. This could include images and words that symbolize your strengths, your struggles, and your hopes for the future.

_____

_____

_____

_____

_____

_____

_____

_____

_____

_____

Write a letter to the person who has caused you the most harm through verbal abuse, expressing your feelings and forgiving them. This can be a powerful step in the process of healing and moving forward.

_____

_____

_____

_____

_____

_____

_____

CHAPTER 7: THE IMPACT OF VERBAL ABUSE ON THE VICTIMS

Verbal abuse can have a profound and lasting impact on its victims. It can erode a person's self-esteem, confidence, and mental health, leaving them feeling powerless, worthless, and hopeless. It can cause a wide range of physical and emotional symptoms, including depression, anxiety, insomnia, and chronic pain.

Victims of verbal abuse often feel trapped in a cycle of abuse, unable to escape the constant barrage of hurtful words. They may feel like they are walking on eggshells, always afraid of saying or doing something that will trigger another outburst of anger or criticism. This constant state of stress and anxiety can take a toll on a person's mental and physical health, leading to a host of health problems.

Verbal abuse can also have a profound impact on a person's relationships. Victims may find it difficult to trust others and may isolate themselves, cutting off relationships with friends and family members. They may feel like they are unworthy of love and affection, and may struggle to form new relationships.

The effects of verbal abuse can linger long after the abuse has ended. Victims may struggle with feelings of low self-esteem, guilt, and shame, and may struggle to forgive themselves and others. They may also struggle with anxiety and depression, and may struggle to move forward in their lives.

It is important to remember that victims of verbal abuse are not to blame for the abuse they have suffered. The blame lies solely with the abuser, who has chosen to use words as a weapon to hurt and control others. It is also important to understand that healing and recovery are possible, and that with the right support and resources, victims of verbal abuse can find a way to reclaim their power and voice.

In conclusion, it is crucial for society to be more aware of the impact of verbal abuse on its victims, and to work towards preventing it from happening. By providing support and resources to victims, and by raising awareness about the issue of verbal abuse, we can help to empower individuals who have been affected and help them to find a path towards healing and recovery.

A survivor's story

As a child, I was always looking for ways to fit in and be popular. When I got to middle school, I found myself hanging out with the "it" crowd and doing whatever it took to keep their approval. One of the things they enjoyed doing was teasing and taunting other kids at school, and I went along with it to be accepted.

I never really thought about the harm I was causing, and I convinced myself that it was just harmless fun. But that all changed when I met my wife. She opened up to me about the verbal abuse she suffered at the hands of her father, and for the first time, I realized the true impact that my words had on the kids I used to torment.

Looking back, I am filled with regret and shame for the way I treated others. I never intended to cause harm, but I understand now that my words had a profound effect on the people I targeted. I am so sorry to anyone who I may have hurt, and I am grateful to my wife for showing me a different way of thinking and treating others with kindness and respect.

I hope that by sharing my story, others can learn from my mistakes and understand the true impact of their words. Verbal abuse may seem like harmless teasing, but the effects can be long-lasting and devastating. It is important for us all to think about the words we use and the impact they have on those around us.

Journal exercises

Reflection on past experiences: Write about a time when you may have used verbal abuse towards others, either intentionally or unintentionally. How did it make the other person feel? How does it make you feel now, looking back on the situation?

_____

_____

_____

_____

_____

_____

_____

_____

_____

_____

Understanding the impact: Imagine yourself in the shoes of a victim of verbal abuse. How would the words and actions of the abuser affect you?

_____

_____

_____

_____

_____

_____

_____

_____

How would it impact your self-esteem, confidence, and mental health?

_____

_____

_____

_____

_____

_____

_____

_____

_____

_____

_____

Empathy building: Think of someone in your life who may have been a victim of verbal abuse, or someone you know who is currently experiencing it. Write a letter to them expressing your empathy and support.

_____

_____

_____

_____

_____

_____

_____

_____

_____

Self-care and self-compassion: Write down a list of positive affirmations and self-care practices you can use when you're feeling overwhelmed by negative thoughts or emotions related to past experiences with verbal abuse.

_____

_____

_____

_____

_____

_____

_____

_____

_____

_____

_____

Forgiveness and growth: Write about a situation where you had to forgive someone for verbal abuse they may have inflicted on you. How did it impact your journey towards healing and recovery? How did it shape you into the person you are today?

_____

_____

_____

_____

_____

_____

_____

_____

_____

_____

CHAPTER 8: HOW VERBAL ABUSE CAN AFFECT SELF-ESTEEM, CONFIDENCE, AND MENTAL HEALTH

As a survivor of verbal abuse, I know firsthand how devastating its effects can be on an individual's self-esteem, confidence, and mental health. For years, I lived with the constant barrage of hurtful words and criticism from my abuser, not realizing the toll it was taking on me. I felt ashamed, worthless, and powerless, and struggled to believe in myself and my abilities.

The impact of verbal abuse on self-esteem is perhaps one of its most devastating effects. Constant criticism and belittlement can leave victims feeling insecure and inadequate, causing them to question their abilities and worth as a person. This can be especially damaging for individuals who are already struggling with low self-esteem, as it can reinforce negative beliefs and further erode their confidence.

Verbal abuse can also have a profound impact on an individual's confidence. Constant criticism and negativity can leave victims feeling unsure of themselves, causing them to doubt their decisions and abilities. This can lead to feelings of anxiety and fear, making it difficult for them to take risks and pursue their goals.

The effects of verbal abuse on mental health can be equally devastating. The constant barrage of hurtful words can leave victims feeling overwhelmed and stressed, leading to symptoms of depression, anxiety, and other mental health disorders. In some cases, verbal abuse can even lead to thoughts of suicide, as victims feel hopeless and helpless in the face of their abuser's cruelty.

Despite the devastating effects of verbal abuse, I have learned that recovery is possible. With the help of supportive friends, family, and mental health professionals, I have been able to work through the pain and trauma of my past experiences. I have learned to believe in myself again, and to understand that I am worthy of love and respect.

If you are a victim of verbal abuse, or if you know someone who is, know that there is hope and help available. You do not have to live with the pain and trauma of verbal abuse any longer. With the right support and resources, you can reclaim your power and voice, and find a path towards healing and recovery.

A Survivors Story

As a survivor of verbal abuse, I know all too well the devastating impact it can have on one's self-esteem, confidence, and mental health. Growing up, I was constantly belittled and criticized by my partner, who used their words as weapons to tear me down and control me. At first, I didn't realize what was happening. I thought their negative words were just their way of expressing concern or displeasure. But as time went on, their constant barrage of insults and accusations began to take its toll on me.

I started to feel like I was never good enough, that I was always failing. My self-esteem plummeted and I lost all confidence in myself. I felt like I was trapped in a cycle of abuse, constantly trying to please my partner but never being able to do enough to escape their wrath. The constant verbal abuse began to wear on my mental health as well. I felt anxious and depressed all the time, and I struggled to see a way out.

It wasn't until I started talking to my therapist that I realized what was happening to me was not okay. My therapist helped me to see the damaging effects of verbal abuse and how it was impacting my life. With their support and guidance, I was able to find the strength to leave the relationship and start my journey towards healing and recovery.

The road to recovery was not easy, but with the help of my therapist and my loved ones, I was able to begin to rebuild my self-esteem and confidence. I learned that my worth is not determined by what others say about me, and that I have the power to choose how I react to negative words.

Today, I am proud to say that I am a survivor of verbal abuse. I have come out on the other side stronger and more resilient, and I am committed to spreading the message of hope to others who are still struggling. No one deserves to be verbally abused, and with the right support and resources, anyone can overcome it and reclaim their power and voice.

Journal exercises

Reflect on your own experiences with verbal abuse, if any. Write down specific instances and the impact they had on you.

_____

_____

_____

_____

_____

_____

_____

_____

_____

_____

Imagine a life without verbal abuse. Write down what that would look like, and how it would make you feel.

_____

_____

_____

_____

_____

_____

_____

_____

_____

_____

Write a letter to yourself, from the perspective of your future self, who is free from verbal abuse and has overcome its effects.

_____

_____

_____

_____

_____

_____

_____

_____

_____

_____

_____

_____

_____

_____

Write a letter to the person who engaged in verbal abuse towards you, expressing your feelings and experiences. This can be a cathartic exercise, even if you do not choose to share the letter with the person.

_____

_____

_____

_____

_____

_____

_____

_____

_____

_____

_____

_____

_____

_____

_____

_____

_____

_____

_____

_____

Write a dialogue between yourself and a trusted friend or counselor, discussing your experiences with verbal abuse and your path towards healing and recovery.

_____

_____

_____

_____

_____

_____

_____

_____

_____

_____

_____

Write a list of affirmations that you can use to boost your self-esteem and counteract the negative effects of verbal abuse.

_____

_____

_____

_____

_____

_____

_____

_____

_____

Write a list of actions that you can take to protect yourself from verbal abuse, and to empower yourself in the face of it.

_____

_____

_____

_____

_____

_____

_____

_____

_____

_____

_____

Write about a time when you stood up for yourself or someone else against verbal abuse. Reflect on the impact this had, and how it made you feel.

_____

_____

_____

_____

_____

_____

_____

_____

_____

Write a personal plan for healing and recovery, focusing on specific steps you can take to address the effects of verbal abuse on your self-esteem, confidence, and mental health.

_____

_____

_____

CHAPTER 9: THE REASONS BEHIND WHY PEOPLE ENGAGE IN VERBAL ABUSE

Verbal abuse is a serious issue that can have a lasting impact on individuals, but why do some people engage in this harmful behavior? Understanding the reasons behind why people engage in verbal abuse is an important step towards preventing it and helping those who have been affected by it.

There are several reasons why people engage in verbal abuse, some of which are rooted in psychological, emotional, and social factors. For example, some individuals engage in verbal abuse as a way to exert power and control over others. This behavior may be the result of childhood experiences where they were taught to be controlling or to use words to get what they want. In other cases, verbal abuse may be a symptom of deeper emotional issues, such as anger, jealousy, or insecurity.

Another reason why people engage in verbal abuse is because they lack the skills necessary to communicate effectively and resolve conflicts in a healthy manner. They may not have learned healthy coping mechanisms for dealing with their emotions, or they may have learned abusive behaviors from their own parents or other authority figures. In these cases, verbal abuse can be a manifestation of deeper emotional and psychological issues.

Verbal abuse can also be driven by cultural and societal factors. Some cultures and communities may be more accepting of abusive language, or may even consider it a normal part of daily life. Additionally, some people may engage in verbal abuse as a way to cope with stress or to alleviate feelings of boredom or frustration.

In conclusion, the reasons behind why people engage in verbal abuse are complex and can vary from person to person. However, it is important to understand the root causes of this behavior so that we can work towards preventing it and helping those who have been affected by it. By creating a more empathetic and understanding society, we can work towards reducing the prevalence of verbal abuse and promoting healthier relationships.

Survivor's Story:

My name is Eva and I am a survivor of verbal abuse. Growing up, I never realized the power of words and how they can impact a person's self-esteem, confidence, and mental health. It wasn't until I met my first husband, who used words to break me down little by little, that I understood the true impact of verbal abuse.

I often wondered why my husband felt the need to belittle me and use hurtful words. It wasn't until I started therapy and did some self-reflection that I realized he engaged in verbal abuse because of his own insecurities and need for control. He wanted to make himself feel better by tearing me down and making me feel small.

It wasn't until I left that toxic relationship that I started to understand the reasons behind why people engage in verbal abuse. It can stem from a lack of emotional regulation, past experiences of trauma or abuse, low self-esteem, or a desire for power and control over others.

It took a lot of time and work, but I was able to heal and reclaim my power. I now understand that my worth and value come from within, and no one can take that away from me with their words.

I share my story to raise awareness about the reasons behind verbal abuse and to show others that it is possible to heal and find a way forward. If you or someone you know is experiencing verbal abuse, I encourage you to seek help and support. You are not alone, and you deserve to live a life free from hurtful words.

Journal Exercises

Reflection on personal experiences: Take a few moments to reflect on any instances in your life where you have been the victim or the perpetrator of verbal abuse. Write down your thoughts and feelings about these experiences.

_____

_____

_____

_____

_____

_____

_____

_____

_____

_____

_____

_____

_____

_____

_____

_____

_____

_____

Understanding your triggers: Write down the specific words or phrases that trigger you and the emotions that come up for you when you hear them. Try to understand why these words or phrases have such an impact on you.

_____

_____

_____

_____

_____

_____

_____

_____

_____

_____

_____

_____

_____

_____

_____

_____

_____

_____

_____

The power of words: Write a list of positive words or phrases that you would like to hear more often. Reflect on how these words or phrases make you feel and what kind of impact they have on your self-esteem and confidence.

_____

_____

_____

_____

_____

_____

_____

_____

_____

_____

_____

_____

_____

_____

_____

_____

_____

_____

_____

The role of mindfulness: Practice mindfulness by taking a few moments to focus on your breath and let go of any distracting thoughts or feelings. Write down how this exercise makes you feel and what kind of impact it has on your ability to manage stress and negativity.

_____

_____

_____

_____

_____

_____

_____

_____

_____

_____

_____

_____

_____

_____

_____

_____

_____

_____

_____

Building resilience: Write down the ways in which you can build resilience against verbal abuse, such as seeking support from loved ones, practicing self-care, and learning to set healthy boundaries.

_____

_____

_____

_____

_____

_____

_____

_____

_____

_____

_____

_____

_____

_____

_____

_____

_____

_____

_____

_____

Gratitude journal: Write down three things that you are
grateful for each day. Reflect on how these positive
experiences can help counteract the negative effects of verbal
abuse.

_____

_____

_____

_____

_____

_____

_____

_____

_____

_____

_____

_____

_____

_____

_____

_____

_____

_____

_____

PART 3: THE SURVIVOR'S JOURNEY

Verbal abuse can leave a profound and lasting impact on its victims, affecting their self-esteem, confidence, and mental health. But amidst the pain and turmoil, there is hope. The journey towards healing and recovery is a difficult one, but it is a journey that many survivors have taken and come out stronger on the other side. This section is dedicated to the survivors of verbal abuse, to their courage and resilience, and to the hope that there is a brighter future ahead.

The Survivor's Journey is a testament to the strength and resilience of the human spirit. It is a journey of self-discovery, growth, and empowerment. It is a journey of overcoming fear, shame, and self-doubt. It is a journey of finding the courage to seek help, to take back control of your life, and to begin the process of healing and recovery.

This section will provide an overview of the survivor's experience with verbal abuse, explore the struggles they face with self-doubt, fear, and shame, and examine the important decision to seek help and begin their journey to healing. The stories of hope and resilience in these chapters will serve as a source of inspiration and encouragement for those who are currently on the same path.

So, to all the survivors of verbal abuse, know that you are not alone, and that there is hope. Your journey towards healing and recovery is a testament to your strength, and with the right support and guidance, you will find your way forward.

The Survivor's Journey

Words can be weapons, so cruel and so mean,
Leaving wounds that are deep and unseen.
They shatter confidence, and rob you of peace,
Making you feel like you're lost and alone, and will
never be released.

But you're a survivor, with a strength that runs deep,
And you've chosen to rise from the ashes, from the
wounds that were left to heal.
With each step, you're rebuilding your self-esteem,
And reclaiming your power, the one that they tried to
steal.

The journey may be long and filled with strife,
But you're determined to heal and to live a life that is
rich and full.
You'll face your fears, your doubts, and your shame,
And you'll emerge stronger, braver, and beautiful.

So hold on tight, to the hope that you've found,
And never forget that you're never alone, never lost,
never down.
With each breath, you'll reclaim your voice,
And you'll be a beacon of hope, a symbol of strength,
and a source of joy and rejoice

CHAPTER 10: OVERVIEW OF THE SURVIVOR'S EXPERIENCE WITH VERBAL ABUSE

Verbal abuse is a form of emotional abuse that can leave deep scars on a person's soul. It's a journey that can feel endless and overwhelming, one where the survivor is constantly grappling with self-doubt, fear, and shame. Despite this, they remain determined to heal and reclaim their power.

The experience of verbal abuse is a complex one, often starting with small insults or demeaning comments. Over time, these insults can escalate, becoming more frequent and more damaging to the victim's self-esteem and confidence. The survivor may feel trapped, as if there is no escape from the constant barrage of negative words and hurtful accusations.

For many survivors, the experience of verbal abuse is like a living nightmare. They may feel isolated, as if no one understands what they're going through. They may feel like they are walking on eggshells, always afraid of setting off the abuser. They may feel like they are losing their mind, as their once confident and secure self is gradually worn down.

The impact of verbal abuse on a survivor's mental and emotional health can be devastating. They may suffer from anxiety and depression, struggling to find joy and purpose in their life. They may struggle with self-doubt, constantly questioning their own worth and abilities. They may feel ashamed, as if the abuse is a reflection of their own shortcomings.

Despite all of this, survivors of verbal abuse are incredibly strong and resilient. They possess an inner strength that allows them to keep going, even in the face of seemingly insurmountable obstacles. They are determined to heal and reclaim their power, to break free from the cycle of abuse and find a brighter future. This is their journey, one filled with courage, strength, and hope.

Journal Exercises

Reflection Exercise: Write about your own experiences with verbal abuse. Have you ever been a victim of verbal abuse, either from someone close to you or from someone at work or school?

_____

_____

_____

_____

_____

_____

_____

_____

_____

_____

How did it make you feel at the time, and how do those feelings still impact you now?

_____

_____

_____

_____

_____

_____

_____

_____

_____

Self-Care Exercise: Make a list of things that make you feel good about yourself. These can be simple things like taking a long bath, reading a book, or going for a walk in nature. Choose one or two items from your list and do them today, taking time to focus on your own self-care and well-being.

_____

_____

_____

_____

_____

_____

_____

_____

_____

_____

Gratitude Exercise: Write down three things you are grateful for today. These can be big or small things, but the point is to focus on what is going well in your life and to find moments of positivity and joy.

_____

_____

_____

_____

_____

_____

_____

_____

_____

Empowerment Exercise: Write a letter to yourself, affirming your strengths, your resilience, and your ability to overcome adversity. Remind yourself of your worth and the things that make you special and unique.

_____

_____

_____

_____

_____

_____

_____

_____

_____

_____

_____

_____

_____

_____

_____

_____

_____

_____

_____

_____

_____

_____

_____

_____

_____

_____

_____

_____

_____

Mindfulness Exercise: Spend some time practicing mindfulness meditation. This can involve simply focusing on your breath and letting thoughts come and go without getting caught up in them. The goal is to be present in the moment and to find peace and stillness within yourself.

_____

_____

_____

_____

_____

_____

_____

_____

_____

Self-Reflection Exercise: Write down your thoughts and feelings about the journey towards healing from verbal abuse. What fears or obstacles do you anticipate facing, and how do you plan to overcome them?

_____

_____

_____

_____

_____

_____

_____

_____

What strengths and resources do you bring to the journey, and how will you support yourself along the way?

Self-Expression Exercise: Find a creative outlet for expressing your thoughts and feelings about your experiences with verbal abuse. This could be through writing, art, music, or another form of self-expression that resonates with you. Allow yourself to express your emotions and thoughts in a safe and healing way.

_____

_____

_____

_____

_____

_____

_____

_____

_____

_____

_____

_____

_____

_____

_____

_____

_____

_____

_____

_____

_____

_____

_____

CHAPTER 11: THE SURVIVOR'S STRUGGLES WITH SELF-DOUBT, FEAR, AND SHAME

For many survivors of verbal abuse, the journey to healing and recovery is often fraught with emotions such as self-doubt, fear, and shame. These feelings can be particularly overwhelming as they can stem from a deep-seated belief that the abuse was their fault, that they are to blame for what happened. It can be difficult for survivors to shake these negative thoughts and feelings, especially when they are the result of years of being told they are not good enough, that they don't deserve love or respect.

Survivors of verbal abuse often struggle with feelings of self-doubt, constantly questioning their own abilities, decisions, and worth. They may feel like they are walking on eggshells, constantly afraid of making a mistake or saying the wrong thing. This self-doubt can make it difficult for survivors to assert themselves, to speak up for themselves, or to trust their own instincts. It can also cause them to question their own memory and perception of events, leaving them feeling confused and uncertain about what is real and what is not.

Fear is another common emotion experienced by survivors of verbal abuse. Fear can manifest in many ways, from a constant sense of unease and anxiety to physical symptoms such as sweating, shaking, and heart palpitations. The fear can stem from a belief that the abuse will happen again, that they will be hurt or hurt someone else, or that they will never be able to escape the abuse. This fear can make it difficult for survivors to move forward and can hold them back from pursuing their goals and dreams.

Shame is another emotion that survivors of verbal abuse often struggle with. The abuser can feel ashamed of what happened to them, that they allowed it to happen, and that they were not strong enough to stop it. This shame can cause survivors to feel like they have to hide what happened, to pretend everything is okay, even when it's not. This can lead to feelings of isolation and loneliness, as survivors feel like they cannot confide in anyone about what they are going through.

In conclusion, self-doubt, fear, and shame are common struggles for survivors of verbal abuse. These feelings can be overwhelming and can hold survivors back from healing and moving forward. It is important for survivors to recognize these feelings and to seek support and guidance as they work towards overcoming them. With the right resources and support, survivors can find a way to reclaim their power, to heal, and to move forward with confidence and hope.

The journey to healing, a road so tough,
A path filled with self-doubt, fear, and rough.

A survivor's experience, with verbal abuse,
A weight on their shoulder, they can't diffuse.

The scars of the past, a constant reminder,
Of the hurtful words, so unkind and imprudent.
A voice that echoes, the insults so vile,
Breaking down the self-esteem, making them feel so small.

Shame creeps in, like a thief in the night,
Stealing the joy and the hope in sight.
Leaving the survivor, feeling alone,
With a burden they bear, all on their own.

But hope shines bright, in the darkest of days,
A glimmer of light, to lead the way.
A journey to healing, a path so true,
With the strength to overcome, and start anew.

Journal Exercises

Write about a time when you felt self-doubt or fear.

_____

_____

_____

_____

_____

_____

_____

_____

_____

What was the situation and what were the thoughts or feelings that came up for you?

_____

_____

_____

_____

_____

_____

_____

_____

_____

How did you cope with these feelings?

_____

_____

_____

_____

_____

_____

_____

_____

_____

Reflect on any moments of shame that you have experienced as a result of verbal abuse. What were the specific circumstances and what were the thoughts and feelings that came up for you at the time?

_____

_____

_____

_____

_____

_____

_____

_____

_____

Think about a time when you felt confident and in control. Write about the experience, what you did and what you felt.

_____

_____

_____

_____

_____

_____

_____

_____

How did this experience impact you?

_____

_____

_____

_____

_____

_____

_____

_____

_____

_____

_____

Write a letter to yourself, addressing the fears and doubts that you have had since experiencing verbal abuse. Offer yourself comfort and encouragement, and remind yourself of your strengths and the progress that you have made.

_____

_____

_____

_____

_____

_____

_____

_____

_____

Write about a moment when you felt proud of yourself.

_____

_____

_____

_____

_____

_____

_____

_____

_____

_____

What was the situation and what did you do that made you feel proud?

_____

_____

_____

_____

_____

_____

_____

How did this experience impact your sense of self-worth and confidence?

_____

_____

_____

_____

_____

_____

_____

_____

Write about a time when you received support from someone else. Who was it and what did they do to help you? How did this experience impact you and your sense of self-worth?

Reflect on any negative self-talk that you have experienced since experiencing verbal abuse.

_____
_____
_____
_____
_____
_____
_____
_____
_____
_____

What are the specific thoughts or beliefs that come up for you, and how do they make you feel?

_____
_____
_____
_____
_____
_____
_____
_____
_____

Write a letter to the person who subjected you to verbal abuse, addressing the pain and suffering that their words caused you. Express your anger and disappointment, but also offer forgiveness and a wish for them to find healing and peace.

_____

_____

_____

_____

_____

_____

_____

_____

_____

_____

_____

_____

_____

_____

_____

_____

_____

_____

_____

_____

Reflect on your journey towards healing and recovery so far. Write about the challenges you have faced, the progress you have made, and your hopes for the future.

_____

_____

_____

CHAPTER 12: THE SURVIVOR'S DECISION TO SEEK HELP AND BEGIN THEIR JOURNEY TO HEALING

For many survivors of verbal abuse, the decision to seek help and begin their journey towards healing can be both daunting and liberating. After experiencing such toxic and harmful words from someone they loved and trusted, it can be difficult to come to terms with the reality of the abuse and the impact it has had on their self-esteem, confidence, and mental health. The fear of being judged, not believed, or not understood can be overwhelming, leading many survivors to stay silent and suffer in silence.

However, despite the fear and doubts, there is a glimmer of hope. A voice inside the survivor's mind that whispers, "You deserve better. You deserve to be loved and respected. You deserve to heal." This voice may be small at first, but as the survivor begins to listen to it, it becomes louder and clearer, inspiring them to take the first step towards recovery.

For some, that first step may be talking to a trusted friend or family member. For others, it may be reaching out to a therapist or support group. Whatever form it takes, the decision to seek help is a brave and courageous one, and marks the beginning of a long and challenging journey towards healing.

On this journey, the survivor will face many obstacles, including self-doubt, fear, and shame. They will be forced to confront the pain and trauma they have experienced, and to challenge the negative thoughts and beliefs that the abuse has instilled in them. They will need to find the strength to rebuild their shattered self-esteem and confidence, and to reclaim their power and voice.

But despite the difficulties, the journey towards healing is also filled with moments of hope and triumph. The survivor will learn to love and accept themselves for who they are, to trust again, and to believe in their own strength and resilience. They will form new relationships based on love, respect, and mutual support, and will find the courage to break the cycle of abuse, both for themselves and for future generations.

So, for anyone who is a survivor of verbal abuse, know that you are not alone. Your experiences are valid, and your pain is real. And, most importantly, know that with the right support and guidance, you can overcome the challenges of your journey towards healing and reclaim the life you deserve.

A survivor's story

Meet Jessica, a 32-year-old woman who grew up in a loving family and never thought she would find herself in a situation like this. Jessica had been married to her high school sweetheart for 8 years when she started to notice a change in their relationship. Her husband, who she had always thought was kind and gentle, had begun to use words as weapons. He would belittle her, criticize her, and make her feel like she was not good enough.

At first, Jessica tried to brush it off and tell herself that he didn't mean it. But as the years went by, the verbal abuse became more frequent and more severe. She started to feel like she was walking on eggshells, constantly trying to avoid triggering her husband's anger. Her self-esteem and confidence were shattered, and she found herself feeling isolated, confused, and ashamed.

Despite the abuse, Jessica stayed with her husband, convinced that things would get better. But they only continued to get worse, until one day she reached her breaking point. She realized that she could no longer live like this, that she deserved to be treated with kindness and respect, and that she needed to take control of her life.

Making the decision to leave her husband and seek help was not easy for Jessica. She was filled with fear and self-doubt, and she felt ashamed for staying in the abusive relationship for so long. But with the support of her family and friends, she found the strength to reach out for help.

Jessica began to attend therapy, where she worked through the pain and trauma of her past. She learned about the effects of verbal abuse and how it can impact a person's self-esteem, confidence, and mental health. She started to reclaim her power and voice, and she began to heal from the inside out.

It was a long and difficult journey, but with the support of her therapist and her loved ones, Jessica was able to find her way back to a life filled with hope and happiness. She realized that she was not to blame for the abuse, and that she had the power to create a new and better life for herself.

Today, Jessica is a confident and strong woman who is proud of her journey to healing. She is an advocate for survivors of verbal abuse, and she shares her story in hopes of helping others find their way forward. Her message is one of hope and resilience, reminding us all that it is possible to overcome the effects of verbal abuse and reclaim our power and voice.

Journal Exercises

Reflection Exercise: Write a letter to your inner self, addressing the feelings and experiences you have been through as a result of verbal abuse. Share with yourself what you need to heal and how you can support yourself in this journey.

_____

_____

_____

_____

_____

_____

_____

_____

_____

_____

Gratitude Practice: Write down three things you are grateful for each day and reflect on how these things have helped you in your journey towards healing.

_____

_____

_____

_____

_____

_____

_____

_____

_____

Affirmations: Write a list of affirmations that reflect your strengths, values, and beliefs. Repeat these affirmations to yourself each day, as a way to counteract negative self-talk.

_____

_____

_____

_____

_____

_____

_____

_____

_____

_____

Creative Expression: Choose a form of creative expression that resonates with you (such as journaling, drawing, painting, or writing poetry) and use it to express your emotions and experiences.

_____

_____

_____

_____

_____

_____

_____

_____

_____

Mindfulness Meditation: Practice mindfulness meditation for at least 10 minutes each day. Focus on your breath and let go of any thoughts or feelings that arise.

_____

_____

_____

_____

_____

_____

_____

_____

_____

_____

_____

Forgiveness Practice: Write a letter of forgiveness to someone who has hurt you through verbal abuse, including yourself if you have also engaged in verbal abuse. Reflect on the feelings that come up during this exercise and use it as a way to release anger and resentment

_____

_____

_____

_____

_____

_____

_____

_____

_____

_____

_____

_____

_____

_____

_____

_____

_____

_____

_____

_____

_____

Gratitude Jar: Start a gratitude jar and write down things you are grateful for each day. When you feel low, read the jar to remind yourself of the positive things in your life.

_____

_____

_____

_____

_____

_____

_____

_____

_____

Self-Care Checklist: Create a self-care checklist that includes activities that help you feel good about yourself, both physically and mentally. Make sure to prioritize these activities and make time for them in your daily routine.

_____

_____

_____

_____

_____

_____

_____

_____

_____

_____

_____

Support Network: Write down the names of people who support and encourage you, and reflect on why they are important in your life. Use this list to reach out to these individuals when you need help and support.

Inner Strength: Reflect on moments when you have demonstrated inner strength, and use these memories as a source of inspiration and motivation. Write down what you have learned from these experiences and how you can apply them to your journey towards healing.

PART 4
OVERCOMING
VERBAL ABUSE

The road to healing from verbal abuse is long and arduous, but it is a journey worth taking. The scars of verbal abuse run deep, affecting our self-esteem, confidence, and mental health. But with the right support, resources, and determination, it is possible to overcome the impact of verbal abuse and reclaim our power and voice.

In Part 4 of this guide, we delve into the various steps of overcoming verbal abuse. We will explore the importance of recognizing the signs of verbal abuse, building self-esteem and self-worth, setting boundaries with the abuser, and learning how to communicate effectively. We will also discuss the importance of seeking support from friends, family, or professionals to help us on our journey towards healing.

The journey towards recovery can be difficult, but it is a journey filled with hope and possibility. With each step we take, we become stronger and more resilient. And as we begin to heal, we reclaim our voice and our power, allowing us to live a life free from the damaging effects of verbal abuse.

CHAPTER 13: RECOGNIZING THE SIGNS OF VERBAL ABUSE

As a researcher, storyteller, and champion of vulnerability, Brené Brown knows the power of words and the impact they can have on our lives. In this chapter, we delve into the often-unrecognized signs of verbal abuse, and how they can have a lasting impact on our self-esteem, confidence, and mental health.

Verbal abuse can often be insidious, creeping into our lives in ways that we may not even realize. It can be disguised as jokes, criticism, or manipulation, but the impact it has on the victim is all too real. From constant belittling and criticism, to name-calling and humiliation, verbal abuse can chip away at our self-worth, leaving us feeling small, broken, and unsure of our place in the world.

It is important to recognize the signs of verbal abuse, and to understand that they are not always obvious. Verbal abuse can take many forms, from subtle put-downs and sarcasm, to more overt forms of aggression like yelling, screaming, or making threats. Whatever the form it takes, it is always damaging and can leave deep scars that can last a lifetime.

As Brené Brown has noted, "Words are containers for power. They can empower or disempower us, depending on how we use them." If you are experiencing any of the signs of verbal abuse, it is important to seek help and begin the journey towards healing and recovery. Whether that means reaching out to friends and family, seeking the support of a therapist or counselor, or simply taking steps to prioritize your own well-being, you have the power to take control of your life and heal from the pain of verbal abuse.

It can be difficult to recognize the signs of verbal abuse, especially if it has been a part of your life for a long time. But remember, you are not alone, and there is help available. By taking the first step towards recognizing the signs of verbal abuse, you are taking the first step towards reclaiming your power and finding a path towards healing and recovery.

Verbal abuse can often be difficult to recognize, especially if it's a pattern of behavior that's become normalized in our relationships. However, it is important to be aware of the warning signs in order to protect ourselves from further harm. Here are some of the often-unrecognized signs of verbal abuse:

Put-downs and criticism: Verbal abuse often involves repeated criticism and put-downs that make us feel worthless, stupid, or unlovable.

Name-calling and insults: Name-calling and insults are another common form of verbal abuse, and can range from mild teasing to outright name-calling and ridicule.

Threats and intimidation: Verbal abuse can also involve threats and intimidation, such as threats of physical harm, or making us feel like we have to comply with someone's demands.

Isolation and exclusion: Verbal abuse can involve isolating someone from their friends and family, and limiting their social circle to only include the abuser.

Blame and guilt-tripping: Verbal abuse can involve blaming someone for everything that goes wrong, and making them feel guilty for things that aren't their fault.

The impact of verbal abuse can be long-lasting and profound. It can affect our self-esteem and confidence, making us feel like we are not good enough and causing us to doubt our own abilities. It can also have a negative impact on our mental health, leading to depression, anxiety, and other psychological disorders.

It is important to be aware of these warning signs and to seek help if you are experiencing any of them. By seeking support, we can begin the process of healing and reclaiming our power and self-worth.

Journal Exercises

Write down a list of words or phrases that have been used to hurt or insult you in the past. Reflect on how each of these words made you feel and the impact they had on your self-esteem, confidence, and mental health.

_____

_____

_____

_____

_____

_____

_____

_____

_____

_____

Write a letter to your past self, addressing the times when you were subjected to verbal abuse. Explain what you would have done differently if you could go back in time and what you have learned since then.

_____

_____

_____

_____

_____

_____

_____

_____

_____

_____

_____

_____

_____

_____

_____

_____

_____

_____

_____

_____

_____

_____

_____

_____

_____

_____

_____

_____

Create a visual representation of the journey towards healing and recovery. This could be in the form of a mind map, a collage, or any other creative format. Reflect on the challenges you faced and the strengths you discovered along the way.

_____

_____

_____

_____

_____

_____

_____

_____

_____

_____

_____

_____

Write down a list of affirmations that you want to remind yourself of daily. These affirmations should focus on building your self-esteem, confidence, and mental health.

_____

_____

_____

_____

_____

_____

_____

_____

_____

_____

Write a letter to your abuser, addressing the ways in which they have hurt you through verbal abuse. Explain how their words have impacted you and what you need from them in order to heal and move forward.

_____

_____

_____

_____

_____

_____

_____

Write a letter to yourself, acknowledging your journey
so far and expressing gratitude for the lessons you have
learned. Reflect on the progress you have made and the
strength you have found within yourself.

_____

_____

_____

_____

_____

_____

_____

_____

_____

_____

_____

_____

_____

_____

_____

_____

_____

CHAPTER 14: BUILDING SELF-ESTEEM AND SELF-WORTH

The journey of healing from verbal abuse is a difficult one, but it is one that is worth taking. One of the most important steps in the process is to rebuild your self-esteem and self-worth. The abuser has chipped away at your confidence, leaving you feeling small and insignificant. But it's time to reclaim your power and remember your worth.

It may feel like an impossible task, but with time and effort, you can regain the self-confidence you once had. Here are some exercises that can help you along the way:

Make a list of your strengths and accomplishments. Take time to reflect on the things you are proud of, both big and small. Write them down and keep the list close by to refer to when you need a boost.

Surround yourself with positive and supportive people. Seek out friends and family members who uplift you and make you feel good about yourself. Limit or eliminate your interactions with those who bring you down.

Practice self-care. Take care of your physical, emotional, and mental health. Exercise, eat well, get enough sleep, and engage in activities that bring you joy.

Set realistic and achievable goals. Celebrate your successes, no matter how small they may be. This will help you feel a sense of accomplishment and boost your self-esteem.

Challenge negative self-talk. When you find yourself thinking negative thoughts about yourself, stop and reframe the thought. Replace "I'm a failure" with "I may have not succeeded this time, but I will try again."

Seek out therapy or counseling. A professional can help you work through the impacts of verbal abuse and provide strategies for building self-esteem and self-worth.

Remember, rebuilding your self-esteem and self-worth takes time and effort, but it is possible. You are capable, worthy, and deserving of a life filled with happiness, confidence, and peace.

CHAPTER 15: SETTING BOUNDARIES WITH THE ABUSER

As a survivor of verbal abuse, you have likely experienced a sense of powerlessness and shame. However, reclaiming your power and setting boundaries with your abuser is a critical step on your journey to healing. This can be a daunting task, but it's also an opportunity to demonstrate to yourself and your abuser that you deserve to be treated with respect and dignity.

When it comes to setting boundaries, it's important to start with a clear understanding of what you need and what you are willing to tolerate. This may mean saying no to certain behaviors or interactions, or it may mean setting limits on the frequency or duration of interactions with your abuser.

One of the most challenging aspects of setting boundaries with an abuser is that it requires a significant shift in power dynamics. You are taking a stand for yourself and communicating that you are no longer willing to accept mistreatment. This can be a difficult and emotional process, but it is essential for your well-being and recovery.

One way to help build your confidence and self-esteem as you set boundaries with your abuser is to focus on self-care and self-compassion. This may involve activities such as journaling, meditating, or spending time with friends and family who support and encourage you. It's also important to remember that setting boundaries is a process and not a one-time event. As you continue to work on yourself and heal, your boundaries may evolve and change.

Another critical aspect of setting boundaries is seeking support from others. This may include talking to friends and family, seeking therapy or counseling, or joining a support group. Having others to share your experiences with and to help you stay accountable can be a valuable resource as you navigate this difficult but empowering process.

In conclusion, setting boundaries with your abuser is a critical step on your journey to healing from verbal abuse. By taking a stand for yourself, focusing on self-care and self-compassion, and seeking support from others, you can begin to reclaim your power, build your self-esteem, and move forward on your journey to healing.

Survivor Story

My name is Jane, and I was a victim of verbal abuse for many years. I was in a relationship with a man who I thought loved me, but he constantly belittled me and made me feel worthless. I was too scared to leave him, but I finally found the courage to set boundaries with him.

It was a long and difficult journey, but I knew I couldn't keep living like this. I sought help from a therapist, who taught me how to recognize the signs of verbal abuse and the impact it was having on my self-esteem, confidence, and mental health. I learned that I was worth so much more than the way I was being treated, and I deserved to be in a healthy and loving relationship.

One of the biggest challenges I faced was setting boundaries with my abuser. It was hard to stand up for myself and tell him what I would and wouldn't tolerate, but I knew it was necessary for my own well-being. I practiced communication skills with my therapist and gradually became more confident in expressing my feelings and needs.

Finally, the day came when I was ready to have the difficult conversation with my abuser. I was nervous and scared, but I reminded myself of my worth and the importance of standing up for myself. To my surprise, the conversation went better than I expected. My partner listened to what I had to say, and we were able to come to an understanding about how we would treat each other moving forward.

Although it wasn't easy, setting boundaries with my partner was one of the best decisions I ever made. It allowed me to take back control of my life and start healing from the verbal abuse. I'm now in a much happier and healthier relationship, and I know that I deserve to be treated with love and respect.

Building self-esteem and self-worth can be a difficult journey for survivors of verbal abuse. The constant belittling and negative words from their abuser can take a heavy toll on their self-esteem and leave them feeling worthless and lacking in confidence. However, it is important to remember that these feelings are not a reflection of their worth as a person. They are simply the result of the abuse they have endured.

For many survivors, the road to building self-esteem and self-worth can be a long and winding one, but it is a journey worth taking. The first step is to recognize the impact that the abuse has had on their self-esteem and to acknowledge the negative thoughts and beliefs they have about themselves. It is important to recognize that these thoughts and beliefs are not based in reality and are simply a result of the abuse they have experienced.

Once they have recognized the impact of the abuse, they can begin to take steps to build their self-esteem and self-worth. This may include setting boundaries with the abuser, seeking support from friends, family, or professionals, and engaging in self-care activities such as exercise, hobbies, or therapy. It may also involve learning new skills, taking on new challenges, and exploring new interests to help boost their confidence and sense of self-worth.

One of the most important things that survivors can do is to surround themselves with positive, supportive people who believe in them and encourage them to see their own worth. This can be a powerful source of strength and can help them to overcome the negative thoughts and beliefs that have been instilled in them by their abuser.

Finally, it is important for survivors to be patient and compassionate with themselves as they work towards building their self-esteem and self-worth. This is not a journey that will happen overnight, but with time and effort, they can reclaim their power and find a sense of self-worth that is unshaken by the abuse they have endured.

In the end, the journey to building self-esteem and self-worth is about taking back control of their lives and embracing their own worth and value as a person. It is a journey of hope and healing, and it is a journey that is worth every step.

CHAPTER 16: LEARNING HOW TO COMMUNICATE EFFECTIVELY

For many survivors of verbal abuse, the idea of communicating effectively can seem like a daunting task. The fear of being unheard, dismissed, or even attacked again can be overwhelming. However, learning how to communicate effectively is a crucial part of healing and overcoming the effects of verbal abuse.

As survivors begin to work on building their self-esteem and self-worth, they may find that they are more confident in their ability to communicate their needs and feelings. However, it's important to remember that learning how to communicate effectively takes time, patience, and practice.

One of the first steps in learning how to communicate effectively is becoming aware of your own thoughts, feelings, and beliefs. This means paying attention to what you are telling yourself and recognizing when your internal dialogue is negative or self-critical. For many survivors, negative self-talk is a result of the verbal abuse they have experienced. By recognizing and interrupting these thoughts, survivors can begin to shift their internal dialogue and develop a more positive and self-affirming outlook.

In addition to becoming more self-aware, survivors can also benefit from learning new communication skills and techniques. For example, active listening, assertiveness, and expressing needs and feelings in a healthy and non-confrontational manner can all help survivors to communicate more effectively.

It's important for survivors to remember that communication is a two-way street. By setting clear and healthy boundaries, survivors can ensure that their needs and feelings are being heard and respected by others. This can include saying "no" when necessary, speaking up when they are not being heard, or setting aside time to reflect on their thoughts and feelings before engaging in a difficult conversation.

It can be helpful for survivors to seek support from friends, family, or professionals as they work on improving their communication skills. This can provide a safe and supportive space for survivors to practice their new skills and receive feedback and encouragement as they progress.

In conclusion, learning how to communicate effectively is a key part of the journey towards healing and overcoming the effects of verbal abuse. By becoming more self-aware, practicing new communication skills, and seeking support, survivors can regain their voice, assert their needs and feelings, and build healthy relationships with others.

Survivor's story

Meet Althea. Growing up, Althea never really knew how to communicate effectively. Her parents were always fighting and shouting at each other, and as a result, Althea learned to internalize her emotions and bottle up her feelings. This pattern of behavior continued into her adult life and her relationships.

She found herself constantly frustrated and unable to express herself, especially in her romantic relationships. She would often find herself getting into arguments and fights, with her partners not understanding what she was trying to say.

One day, Althea decided enough was enough. She knew that if she wanted to be truly happy and have healthy relationships, she needed to learn how to communicate effectively. She started reading books, attending workshops, and seeking out therapy to help her improve her communication skills.

The journey wasn't easy, but with time and patience, Althea started to see a change in herself. She became more confident in expressing herself and was able to have much more meaningful conversations with her partners. She learned how to listen to others and be more empathetic, which in turn helped her build stronger relationships.

Now, Althea is a much happier and more fulfilled person. She knows that communication is the key to any successful relationship and is grateful for the journey she went through to get there.

Journal exercises

Reflect on a time when you struggled with effective communication in a relationship. What was the situation and how did you handle it?

_____

_____

_____

_____

_____

_____

_____

_____

_____

_____

Think about a person in your life who you consider to be a great communicator. What are some of the characteristics or qualities that make them an effective communicator?

_____

_____

_____

_____

_____

_____

_____

_____

_____

_____

_____

How could you apply those qualities to your own
communication style?

_____

_____

_____

_____

_____

_____

_____

_____

_____

Write down three of your personal communication
strengths and three areas you would like to improve.

_____

_____

_____

_____

_____

_____

_____

_____

_____

Reflect on a situation where you felt unheard or misunderstood in a conversation. How could you have approached the situation differently to ensure that your thoughts and feelings were effectively communicated?

_____

_____

_____

_____

_____

_____

_____

_____

_____

_____

Identify a person in your life who you struggle to communicate with effectively. Write down three specific communication strategies you could use to improve your interactions with this person.

_____

_____

_____

_____

_____

_____

_____

_____

_____

_____

_____

Reflect on a time when you struggled to express your feelings or thoughts in a healthy and assertive way. Write down what you would do differently in that situation if it were to occur again.

_____

_____

_____

_____

_____

_____

_____

_____

_____

Write a letter to yourself addressing any past experiences with verbal abuse and the steps you have taken or plan to take to improve your communication skills in order to prevent future abuse.

_____

_____

_____

_____

_____

_____

_____

_____

_____

_____

_____

Think about a time when you successfully navigated a difficult conversation. What steps did you take to ensure that both parties were heard and understood?

_____

_____

_____

_____

_____

_____

_____

_____

How did you handle any conflict that arose during the conversation?

_____

_____

_____

_____

_____

_____

_____

_____

_____

Reflect on a time when you used "I" statements in a conversation. How did using "I" statements instead of blaming or accusing language impact the outcome of the conversation?

_____

_____

_____

_____

_____

_____

_____

_____

_____

_____

Write down a list of communication skills and techniques that you would like to practice and improve on, such as active listening, empathy, and assertiveness. Choose one skill to focus on for the next week and journal about your progress and challenges.

CHAPTER 17: SEEKING SUPPORT FROM FRIENDS, FAMILY, OR PROFESSIONALS

When it comes to surviving and overcoming the trauma of verbal abuse, seeking support is crucial. Whether it's from friends, family members, or professionals, having someone to talk to and lean on can make all the difference. For many survivors, taking this step is difficult and overwhelming. They may feel embarrassed, ashamed, or like they're not worthy of help. However, it's important to remember that seeking support is a sign of strength, not weakness. It's a brave step towards healing and reclaiming your life.

One of the first things to keep in mind when seeking support is to find people who you trust and who will listen to you without judgment. This can be difficult for survivors who have experienced abuse, as they may have been told by their abuser that no one would believe them or care about their problems. However, it's important to remember that there are people out there who will believe you, support you, and help you on your journey to healing.

One of the most common forms of support for survivors is therapy. Therapy provides a safe and confidential space for survivors to talk about their experiences and feelings. A therapist can help survivors identify and understand the negative thought patterns and behaviors that have developed as a result of the abuse, and help them develop new, healthy ways of coping. Therapists can also provide survivors with tools and techniques to help them build their self-esteem, confidence, and resilience.

For those who may not feel comfortable with therapy, there are also support groups. Support groups can provide survivors with a community of people who understand what they're going through. They can offer a sense of belonging and validation, as well as opportunities to share experiences, advice, and support.

Friends and family members can also play an important role in a survivor's journey to healing. They can provide emotional support and help survivors feel less isolated and alone. However, it's important to be cautious when seeking support from loved ones, as they may not have the training or experience to effectively support someone who has experienced abuse. In these cases, it may be helpful to refer them to resources such as books or online forums.

In addition to seeking support from people in your life, it's also important to take care of yourself. This may mean engaging in self-care activities, such as exercise, meditation, or hobbies that bring you joy. It may also mean seeking out additional resources, such as books, articles, or online forums, that can provide additional support and guidance.

Remember, seeking support is a critical step in the healing process. Don't be afraid to reach out and ask for help. You are not alone and you deserve to heal and reclaim your life.

Journal Exercise:

Reflect on the support system in your life. Who are the people you trust and feel comfortable reaching out to for support?

_____

_____

_____

_____

_____

_____

_____

_____

_____

Write a list of their names and how they support you.

_____

_____

_____

_____

_____

_____

_____

_____

_____

Think about the different forms of support you may want or need in your journey to healing. This may include therapy, support groups, friends and family members, or self-care activities. Write a list of what you think would be most helpful for you.

Write a letter to yourself outlining your goals for seeking support. This can include what you hope to gain from therapy, what you hope to get out of support groups, or what you hope to achieve through self-care activities.

_____

_____

_____

_____

_____

_____

_____

_____

_____

_____

_____

_____

Make a plan for how you will reach out to the people in your support system. This can include scheduling appointments with a therapist, reaching out to support groups, or talking to friends and family members. Make a plan for how you will make these connections.

PART 5
EMPOWERMENT AND FINDING YOUR VOICE

The journey to healing and empowerment after experiencing verbal abuse can seem overwhelming and impossible, but it is not. It starts with the realization that you are not alone and that you deserve to be treated with respect and dignity. It continues with the process of reclaiming your power and finding your voice. In this section, we will explore the importance of reclaiming your power and the power of voice, and the steps you can take to find your voice and speak up against verbal abuse. We will delve into overcoming the fear of retaliation and building self-confidence, learning how to assert yourself, practicing speaking up and expressing your thoughts and feelings, and building confidence in your voice. Remember, your voice is powerful, and it is time to use it. Embrace your strength and resilience, and let's begin this journey of empowerment and self-discovery together.

CHAPTER 18: UNDERSTANDING THE IMPORTANCE OF RECLAIMING YOUR POWER AND THE POWER OF VOICE

As a survivor of verbal abuse, reclaiming your power can seem like an impossible task. Your self-esteem has been shattered, your confidence has been knocked down, and you may feel like your voice has been taken away from you. However, it is important to understand that reclaiming your power and finding your voice is a critical step in your journey towards healing and empowerment.

The power of your voice is immense. When you use your voice, you assert your presence in the world and send a message that you matter. Your voice is an instrument of self-expression, a way of communicating your thoughts and feelings to others. When you reclaim your voice, you assert your right to be heard and respected. You also assert your right to be treated with dignity and to live a life free of abuse.

Reclaiming your power and finding your voice may not be easy, but it is essential. It requires courage, determination, and a willingness to take action. It requires you to confront your fears and the negative self-talk that may be holding you back. It requires you to embrace your authentic self and to stand up for yourself.

In reclaiming your power and finding your voice, you will start to heal from the wounds of verbal abuse. You will start to rebuild your self-esteem and self-confidence. You will start to feel more in control of your life and your choices. You will start to feel empowered and to live a life of dignity and respect.

Remember, reclaiming your power and finding your voice is a journey, not a destination. It may take time, but it is a journey that is worth taking. You deserve to live a life free of abuse, to be treated with respect, and to have your voice heard. So start your journey today, and never give up on yourself.

A survivor's story

Dear Friend,

I want to share with you my journey of reclaiming my power and finding my voice after experiencing verbal abuse. It was a long and difficult road, but I am now in a much better place, and I hope my story will inspire you to do the same.

I remember feeling completely defeated and hopeless in the aftermath of the abuse. I felt like I had lost all sense of who I was and that my abuser was meaningless. I felt like I had no control over my life, and that I was a prisoner in my own thoughts and feelings.

But I slowly realized that I did have the power to change my situation. I realized that I didn't have to accept the abuse and the negative thoughts it had instilled in me. I could take control of my life again and reclaim my power.

I started by educating myself on verbal abuse and the signs of it. I realized that I had been a victim for a long time, and that I needed to break free from that cycle. I started working on building my self-esteem and self-worth, and I learned to set boundaries with the person who had been abusing me.

I also started seeking support from friends, family, and professionals. I found a therapist who specialized in helping victims of verbal abuse, and I joined a support group. These people helped me see that I was not alone and that there was hope for me.

Finally, I started to find my voice. I started to express my thoughts and feelings and assert myself in situations where I felt threatened. I built up my confidence and overcame my fear of retaliation.

Today, I am a stronger, more confident person, and I no longer allow anyone to treat me with disrespect. I have taken back my power, and I have found my voice. And I know that you can too.

Remember that you deserve to be treated with dignity and respect, and that you have the power to reclaim your life. Take the first step, and don't give up. You are worth it.

With love and support,

Ava

Journal exercises

Reflect on a time when you felt empowered and confident in your own voice. What were the circumstances?

_____

_____

_____

_____

_____

_____

_____

_____

How did you feel? What steps did you take to reach that level of empowerment?

_____

_____

_____

_____

_____

_____

_____

_____

_____

_____

Write down three things you would like to say but have been afraid to voice. Consider why you haven't said these things, and what steps you can take to work through that fear.

_____

_____

_____

_____

_____

_____

_____

_____

_____

Make a list of all the things that make you feel self-doubt or hold you back from speaking up. Write next to each one why you think this is an issue for you and what steps you can take to overcome it.

_____

_____

_____

_____

_____

_____

_____

_____

_____

_____

_____

_____

Write a letter to yourself, acknowledging the strength and resilience you have shown in overcoming verbal abuse. Focus on the positive qualities you possess, and the ways in which you have overcome obstacles to become the person you are today.

_____

_____

_____

_____

_____

_____

_____

_____

_____

_____

_____

_____

_____

_____

_____

_____

_____

_____

_____

_____

_____

_____

_____

_____

Identify a situation in which you felt like your voice wasn't heard. Reflect on why that may have been, and what steps you could have taken to ensure your voice was heard. Consider what you can do in future situations to prevent feeling unheard.

_____

_____

_____

_____

_____

_____

_____

_____

_____

_____

_____

_____

_____

_____

_____

_____

_____

Write down five things you are proud of and five things
you would like to change. Reflect on how you can use your
voice to effect positive change in your life and in the world.

_____

_____

_____

_____

_____

_____

_____

_____

_____

_____

_____

_____

_____

_____

_____

_____

_____

CHAPTER 19 STEPS TO FINDING YOUR VOICE AND SPEAKING UP AGAINST VERBAL ABUSE

Dear survivors,

In this chapter, we'll delve into the steps you can take to find your voice and speak up against verbal abuse. Verbal abuse can have devastating effects on our self-esteem and confidence, making it difficult to speak up and assert ourselves. But it's important to remember that reclaiming your power and speaking your truth is a critical step in your healing journey.

Step 1: Acknowledge the abuse.
The first step in finding your voice is acknowledging that the words and actions of your abuser are indeed abuse. This can be a difficult step, as verbal abuse often sneaks its way into our lives disguised as jokes, insults, or criticism. But it's important to remember that abuse is never okay, and acknowledging it is a crucial step in reclaiming your power.

Step 2: Identify triggers.

Verbal abuse can trigger past traumas or negative beliefs about ourselves. It's important to identify what specific words or actions trigger these feelings, so that you can begin to understand why they affect you and work towards healing.

Step 3: Practice self-care.

Taking care of yourself is essential in building the strength and resilience you need to speak up against abuse. This may include engaging in activities that bring you joy, practicing mindfulness, and seeking support from friends, family, or professionals.

Step 4: Find your support system.

Surrounding yourself with supportive people who believe in you and your worth can be incredibly empowering. This support system can help you work through your fears and insecurities, and give you the courage to speak up against abuse.

Step 5: Learn effective communication skills.

Learning how to communicate effectively can be incredibly empowering, as it allows you to express your thoughts and feelings in a way that is clear and assertive. This can include learning how to set boundaries, how to calmly and respectfully express your opinions, and how to engage in active listening.

Step 6: Practice speaking up.

Speaking up against abuse can be intimidating, but it's important to remember that you don't have to face it alone.

Start by practicing speaking up in small ways, such as expressing your opinions in conversations or standing up for yourself in situations where you feel uncomfortable. As you build confidence in your voice, you'll find that speaking up against abuse becomes easier and more empowering.

These steps may not be easy, but by taking them you can reclaim your power and find your voice. Remember, you are not alone in this journey and there is a bright future ahead of you.

With love and support,

M.L.Ruscsak

CHAPTER 20: OVERCOMING THE FEAR OF RETALIATION AND BUILDING SELF-CONFIDENCE - LEARNING HOW TO ASSERT YOURSELF

Dear reader,

As a survivor of verbal abuse, I understand all too well the fear that can come with speaking up and asserting yourself. The thought of retaliation from your abuser can be overwhelming, making it difficult to find the courage to stand up for yourself. But I'm here to tell you that it is possible to overcome this fear and build self-confidence, and I want to share my journey with you.

When I first realized that I was a victim of verbal abuse, I felt powerless. My self-esteem and confidence had been eroded by my abuser's constant criticism, belittlement, and manipulation. I was afraid to speak up, afraid of the retaliation that might come if I did. I felt trapped, and I didn't know how to break free.

But I knew that if I wanted to heal and move forward, I needed to reclaim my power. I needed to find my voice and speak up. And so, I began the journey to building my self-confidence and overcoming my fear of retaliation.

The first step was to understand that my feelings and thoughts were valid. I needed to acknowledge and accept that what I was experiencing was not my fault, and that I had the right to stand up for myself. This was a difficult step, but it was also an important one. It allowed me to begin to believe in myself and my ability to make a change.

Next, I started to work on building my self-confidence. I took small steps, like trying new things and making decisions for myself, even if they were small ones. I surrounded myself with positive, supportive people who believed in me, and I made a conscious effort to focus on my strengths and accomplishments, rather than my shortcomings.

I also made a plan for how I would handle retaliation if it occurred. I knew that it was a real possibility, and I wanted to be prepared. I sought the support of friends, family, or a professional counselor, who could help me through any difficult situations that might arise.

With time and effort, I learned how to assert myself and speak up against the verbal abuse I was experiencing. I found my voice and used it to advocate for myself and to make changes in my life. And while it wasn't easy, it was worth it. I am now stronger, more confident, and more empowered than ever before.

So, to all the survivors out there, I want you to know that reclaiming your power and building self-confidence is possible. It will take time and effort, but it is worth it. You deserve to live a life free from verbal abuse, and finding your voice is the first step in that journey.

Sincerely,

A Survivor of Verbal Abuse

Journal Exercises

Reflect on a time when you felt like you couldn't speak up for yourself. What was happening in the situation?

_____
_____
_____
_____
_____
_____
_____
_____
_____

What were your thoughts and feelings at the time? How did you react or respond?

_____

_____

_____

_____

_____

_____

_____

_____

_____

_____

Write a list of things that you want to stand up for or speak out against. What are the beliefs or values that motivate you to take this action?

_____

_____

_____

_____

_____

_____

_____

_____

_____

_____

Write a letter to yourself in the future. Imagine that you have overcome the fear of retaliation and have become confident in asserting yourself. What words of encouragement would you like to share with your future self?

_____
_____
_____
_____
_____
_____
_____
_____
_____
_____

What advice would you give to help you get there?

_____
_____
_____
_____
_____
_____
_____
_____
_____
_____

Write a dialogue between you and someone who has wronged you or treated you unfairly. Imagine that you are expressing your thoughts and feelings in a confident and assertive manner. How does the conversation go? How do you feel after the conversation?

_____

_____

_____

_____

_____

_____

_____

_____

_____

_____

Reflect on the things that make you feel confident and empowered. Write a list of these things and how they impact you. Consider how you can cultivate these things in your life to help you build self-confidence and assertiveness.

PART 6 HEALING AND MOVING FORWARD

The journey to healing from verbal abuse is a long and difficult one, but it is also one of the most rewarding and empowering experiences a person can undertake. This part of the journey is about understanding the process of healing, accepting your past experiences, letting go of the pain and hurt, and moving forward with self-love, compassion, and forgiveness.

Verbal abuse can have a profound impact on a person's mental, emotional, and physical well-being. It can leave a person feeling broken, hopeless, and full of self-doubt. The road to recovery can seem overwhelming, but it is important to remember that you are not alone and that there is hope for healing.

In this section, we will explore the role of therapy and support in the healing process, as well as practical strategies for coping with the aftermath of verbal abuse. We will discuss the importance of accepting your past experiences, letting go of the pain and hurt, and moving forward with self-love, compassion, and forgiveness.

Through this process, you will begin to reclaim your power, find your voice, and start to rebuild your self-esteem and confidence. Remember that healing is a journey, and it takes time, patience, and perseverance. But with the right support, resources, and mindset, you can overcome the aftermath of verbal abuse and find peace and happiness in your life.

CHAPTER 21: ACCEPTING YOUR PAST EXPERIENCES

My dear friend, I want to share with you the wisdom that I have learned about the importance of accepting your past experiences. We all carry with us the memories of our past, and for many survivors of verbal abuse, these memories can be particularly painful and difficult to confront.

But I want you to know that accepting your past experiences is a crucial step in the healing process. It is only through acceptance that we can begin to heal the wounds inflicted by verbal abuse. When we refuse to acknowledge the pain and hurt of our past, we only prolong our suffering and prevent ourselves from moving forward.

I understand that accepting your past experiences can be a daunting task, and that it may feel like opening old wounds. But I want you to know that you are not alone, and that there is a way forward.

One of the key things I have learned is that acceptance does not mean that you are condoning the abuse that you experienced. It does not mean that you are forgetting the hurt and pain that you have been through. Rather, it means that you are acknowledging the reality of what happened, and that you are taking the first step towards healing and recovery.

So, I encourage you to be gentle with yourself as you begin this journey. Take your time, and go at your own pace. And remember that there is no right or wrong way to accept your past experiences. What matters most is that you are making the decision to heal and move forward.

I have found that one of the most helpful strategies for accepting your past experiences is to talk about them. Share your story with someone you trust, or seek the support of a therapist or support group. Talking about your experiences can help you process your emotions, and it can also help you feel less alone and isolated.

Another helpful strategy is to practice self-compassion and self-care. Take time for yourself, and do things that make you feel good. Surround yourself with supportive friends and family, and try to focus on the positive things in your life.

And above all, remember that you are a survivor. You are strong, and you are resilient. And with time and patience, you will heal and find the peace and happiness that you deserve.

So, my dear friend, I encourage you to embrace your past experiences with courage and determination. The journey towards healing and acceptance may be difficult, but I promise you that it is worth it. And I believe in you, every step of the way.

Journal exercises

"The Art of Letting Go" - Write down any negative beliefs or thoughts that you have about yourself, your past experiences, or the abuse you suffered. Then, imagine yourself letting go of each thought, one by one, and write down how it feels to let go.

_____

_____

_____

_____

_____

_____

_____

_____

_____

_____

"The Power of Self-Forgiveness" - Write a letter to yourself, forgiving yourself for any mistakes or shortcomings that you feel you may have had in your past experiences with verbal abuse. Acknowledge your strengths and the lessons you've learned, and offer yourself love and compassion.

_____

_____

_____

_____

_____

_____

_____

_____

_____
_____
_____

"The Healing Journey" - Draw a timeline of your life, including significant events and experiences related to verbal abuse. Write down the emotions and thoughts you associate with each event, and then reflect on your journey so far, including any progress you've made towards healing and moving forward.

_____
_____
_____
_____
_____
_____
_____
_____
_____
_____
_____
_____
_____
_____
_____
_____

"Affirmations for Self-Love" - Write a list of positive affirmations that you can repeat to yourself every day. These affirmations should focus on your self-worth, strength, and resilience, and can help you build self-confidence and love for yourself.

_____

_____

_____

_____

_____

_____

_____

_____

_____

_____

_____

_____

_____

_____

_____

_____

_____

_____

"The Future You" - Imagine yourself in the future, free from the pain and hurt of verbal abuse. Write down what you see in your life, including your relationships, career, hobbies, and overall happiness. This exercise can help you focus on the positive aspects of your future and move forward with hope and determination.

_____

_____

_____

_____

_____

_____

_____

_____

_____

_____

_____

_____

_____

_____

_____

_____

_____

_____

CHAPTER 22: LETTING GO OF THE PAIN AND HURT

In this chapter, we will explore the powerful process of letting go of the pain and hurt that has accumulated as a result of verbal abuse. We will take a closer look at the reasons why it can be so difficult to release the negative emotions that we associate with our past experiences and how we can begin to heal and move forward.

We often hold onto our pain and hurt, not just as a result of verbal abuse, but in many areas of our lives. We cling to these feelings because we believe that they are somehow protecting us from future harm. However, this is not the case. Holding onto our pain and hurt only serves to weigh us down and keep us from experiencing joy and peace.

So, how can we begin to let go of the pain and hurt that we have accumulated? The first step is to recognize that we are holding onto these feelings. This may seem like a simple step, but it is actually a powerful one. When we acknowledge the pain and hurt that we are feeling, we can begin to release it.

Next, we can practice self-compassion. This means treating ourselves with kindness and understanding as we work through our emotions. This may involve journaling, practicing self-care, or seeking support from a therapist.

Whatever the method, it is important to be gentle and compassionate with ourselves as we begin to release the pain and hurt that has accumulated.

Another important step in letting go of the pain and hurt is to forgive. This does not mean that we are condoning the abuse we have experienced, but rather that we are releasing the hold that it has over us. Forgiveness can be a challenging process, but it is essential for healing.

Finally, it is important to understand that letting go of the pain and hurt is a journey, not a destination. We will not wake up one day and magically be free of our emotions. However, by taking small steps each day, we can gradually release the pain and hurt that has accumulated and begin to experience peace and joy in our lives.

So, let us embrace this journey of letting go of the pain and hurt that has accumulated as a result of verbal abuse. It is not an easy path, but it is a necessary one. With each step that we take, we will grow stronger, more confident, and more empowered. And in the end, we will find that we have not only released the pain and hurt, but that we have also rediscovered the joy and peace that is our birthright.

A survivor's story

Dear Friend,

It's been a long and difficult journey, but I finally feel like I'm at a place where I can let go of the pain and hurt that has been holding me back for so long. It wasn't easy, but with time, patience, and the support of my loved ones, I've learned to accept what happened to me and move forward in a positive direction.

At first, the thought of letting go of my pain and hurt seemed impossible. The wounds from my past were too deep and the memories were too fresh. But as I took the time to reflect on my experiences and seek support from friends, family, and professionals, I realized that I was capable of letting go and finding peace.

I started by acknowledging my feelings and allowing myself to feel the pain and hurt. This was difficult, but it was also cathartic. I realized that by holding on to my pain, I was only prolonging my suffering. I needed to let go in order to heal and move forward.

I also learned the importance of self-compassion and self-forgiveness. I realized that I wasn't alone in my experiences and that I had nothing to be ashamed of. I also came to understand that I had done the best I could in my situation and that it was time to let go of any feelings of guilt or self-blame.

Now, I feel empowered and ready to continue my journey of healing and growth. I'm not saying that the road ahead will be easy, but I'm confident that with the support of those around me and my newfound strength, I'll be able to overcome any obstacles that come my way.

Sincerely,
A Survivor

Journal Exercises

Reflection on Past Trauma: Write about a specific
traumatic experience related to verbal abuse. Describe the
events, your thoughts and feelings at the time, and how it has
affected you since then.

_____

_____

_____

_____

_____

_____

_____

_____

_____

_____

Identifying Triggers: Make a list of things that trigger
negative emotions or memories related to verbal abuse.
Think about how you can cope with these triggers and work
towards healing.

_____

_____

_____

_____

_____

_____

_____

_____

_____

_____

Forgiveness Letter: Write a letter to yourself or the abuser who verbally abused you. In the letter, express your feelings of hurt, anger, or resentment, and then imagine yourself forgiving them.

_____

_____

_____

_____

_____

_____

_____

_____

_____

_____

Gratitude Journal: Write down three things you are grateful for every day, focusing on the positive things in your life and practicing gratitude.

_____

_____

_____

_____

_____

_____

_____

_____

_____

_____

_____

Mindful Self-Compassion: Spend five minutes each day practicing self-compassion by repeating positive affirmations, such as "I am enough" or "I deserve love and kindness."

_____

_____

_____

_____

_____

_____

_____

_____

_____

Reclaiming Your Power: Write a letter to yourself, reclaiming your power and strength as a survivor of verbal abuse. In the letter, acknowledge your resilience and strength, and commit to moving forward in a positive direction.

CHAPTER 23: THE ROLE OF THERAPY AND SUPPORT IN THE HEALING PROCESS

The journey of healing is not a solitary path, but a delicate dance between the self and the support of others. It is a process that requires patience, persistence, and a willingness to explore the depths of one's soul. It is a path that can be frightening and uncertain, but it is also one of the most rewarding journeys a person can undertake.

Therapy is a valuable tool in the healing process, providing a safe space to unpack and process traumatic experiences. It is an opportunity to work through past hurts and traumas with a trained professional who can offer guidance and support. The therapeutic relationship provides a sounding board for the voice within, a voice that has been silenced for too long. It offers a space for the individual to reclaim their power, to reclaim their voice, and to reclaim their life.

However, therapy is not the only path to healing. Support from friends, family, or support groups can also provide a foundation of love, compassion, and understanding. These supportive relationships offer the individual a safe haven where they can be vulnerable, where they can be seen, and where they can begin to rebuild their self-esteem and confidence.

The journey of healing is not a destination, but a continuous process of growth and self-discovery. It requires a constant commitment to self-care and self-compassion. It is about learning to forgive oneself for past mistakes and to let go of the pain and hurt. It is about learning to love and accept oneself, even in the face of past experiences.

In the end, healing is about reclaiming one's power, reclaiming one's voice, and reclaiming one's life. It is about finding the courage to face the past, to confront the pain and hurt, and to emerge on the other side, stronger and more resilient. It is a journey that requires strength, bravery, and an unwavering commitment to oneself, but it is a journey that is ultimately rewarding.

So let us embrace the journey of healing with open hearts and open minds, knowing that we are not alone, and that there is support available to us every step of the way. Let us find the courage to reclaim our power, to reclaim our voice, and to reclaim our lives. For in the end, it is through healing that we find true empowerment, and it is through empowerment that we find our voice and our place in the world.

Survivor Story

Dear Reader,

I want to take a moment to talk about the importance of therapy and support in the healing process after experiencing verbal abuse. It can be difficult to even consider reaching out for help, but I promise you, it is one of the most powerful and transformative steps you can take towards healing and reclaiming your power.

When we have suffered from verbal abuse, it can be difficult to trust others and feel worthy of support. But I want to remind you that you are deserving of love and care, and that seeking help is a sign of strength, not weakness.

In therapy, you can work with a trained professional to process the emotions and experiences you've been through, and to develop healthy coping mechanisms to support your healing journey. You can learn how to rebuild your self-esteem, set boundaries, and regain a sense of control over your life.

Having a support system of friends and family members who understand and believe in you can also be incredibly valuable. Surrounding yourself with people who lift you up and help you to see your own worth can help to counteract the negative messages you may have internalized from your abuser.

But it's not just about having people in your life who can offer you support; it's also about learning how to support yourself. This is where self-care comes in - by taking care of yourself and filling your life with positive experiences, you can begin to heal from the inside out.

Remember, healing is a journey, and there is no right or wrong way to do it. What matters is that you are making an effort to heal and to build a life that feels true to you. Whether that includes therapy, support groups, or simply taking time to care for yourself, the most important thing is that you are making the choice to heal and move forward in a way that feels right for you.

With love and support,
A survivor

Journal Exercises

Write a letter to your inner child: Think about the child within you who has experienced verbal abuse. Write a letter to that child, offering love, comfort, and reassurance. Reflect on how you can support that inner child and help them to heal.

_____

_____

_____

_____

_____

_____

_____

_____

_____

_____

Reflect on self-care practices: Write down a list of self-care practices that you find helpful in dealing with the aftermath of verbal abuse. Reflect on how these practices have helped you and why they are important to you.

_____

_____

_____

_____

_____

_____

_____

_____

_____

_____

Explore your values and beliefs: Take some time to reflect on your values and beliefs. Write down what you believe about yourself, others, and the world. Reflect on how your beliefs have been affected by your experiences of verbal abuse and how you can start to reclaim your sense of self.

_____

_____

_____

_____

_____

_____

_____

_____

_____

_____

_____

Gratitude journaling: Spend some time each day writing about things you are grateful for. Reflect on the small joys in your life and the ways in which you are supported by those around you.

_____

_____

_____

_____

_____

_____

_____

_____

_____

_____

Reflection on progress: Take some time each week to reflect on the progress you have made in healing from verbal abuse. Write down what you have learned, what you are proud of, and what challenges you have faced. Celebrate your achievements and use this as an opportunity to continue to grow and heal.

CHAPTER 24: STRATEGIES FOR COPING WITH THE AFTERMATH OF VERBAL ABUSE

The aftermath of verbal abuse can be a challenging and overwhelming experience. The scars of emotional pain, low self-esteem, and feelings of worthlessness can last for years, if not a lifetime. It is essential to remember that healing is possible, and there are strategies that can help in coping with the aftermath of verbal abuse. In this chapter, we will explore some of these strategies through the lens of Virginia Woolf's writing style.

A room of one's own

"A woman must have money and a room of her own if she is to write fiction." - Virginia Woolf

In her seminal work, "A Room of One's Own," Virginia Woolf argues that women need both financial and physical independence to fully express themselves and be creative. In a similar vein, those who have experienced verbal abuse need to create a space for themselves, both physically and emotionally. This space should be a safe haven, a place where they can retreat to, process their thoughts, and heal. It can be a physical room, a corner of a room, or even a mental space, but it is essential to have a place where one can be alone and away from the chaos and pain of the past.

Take care of yourself

"Life is not a spectacle or a feast; it is a predicament." - Virginia Woolf

The aftermath of verbal abuse can be a harrowing experience, and it can be easy to neglect oneself. However, self-care is critical to healing. This can include simple acts like taking a relaxing bath, going for a walk, or spending time with friends. It can also involve more structured activities such as therapy or self-help groups. Whatever the form of self-care, it is essential to make time for oneself and prioritize one's well-being.

Re-define your identity

"I am made and remade continually. Different people draw different words from me." - Virginia Woolf

The experience of verbal abuse can leave individuals feeling shattered and unsure of their identity. It is crucial to understand that the abuse does not define who one is and that it is possible to reclaim and re-define one's identity. This process of self-discovery can involve exploring new interests and hobbies, setting new goals and aspirations, or simply taking the time to reflect on who one truly is.

Forgive, but do not forget

"Memory is not a drum; it is a symphony." - Virginia Woolf

Forgiveness is a crucial step in healing from verbal abuse, but it is essential to remember that it does not mean forgetting. Holding onto the pain and hurt of the past can keep one trapped and prevent healing. Forgiveness allows one to release the hold that the past has over them, to move forward, and to heal. However, it is important to keep the memories of the past as a reminder of what one has overcome and as a tool for future growth and healing.

In conclusion, healing from the aftermath of verbal abuse is a long and challenging journey, but it is one that is possible. By taking care of oneself, re-defining one's identity, forgiving but not forgetting, and creating a safe space, individuals can start the process of healing and move forward with self-love, compassion, and forgiveness.

Journal Exercise:

Find a quiet, safe place to reflect and write about your thoughts and feelings related to the aftermath of verbal abuse.
Write a letter to yourself, forgiving yourself for any mistakes or perceived shortcomings that may have contributed to the abuse.

_____
_____
_____
_____
_____
_____
_____
_____

Identify three activities or self-care practices that you can incorporate into your daily routine to help you cope with the aftermath of verbal abuse.

_____
_____
_____
_____
_____
_____
_____
_____
_____
_____

Write in a journal - This activity allows you to reflect on your experiences and emotions, release any pent up frustration, and gain a sense of control over your thoughts.

_____
_____
_____

_____

_____

_____

_____

_____

_____

_____

Engage in mindfulness meditation - Taking a few minutes to focus on your breath and be present in the moment can help you manage stress, anxiety and emotional pain.

Connect with nature - Spending time in nature, whether through hiking, gardening, or simply sitting outside, can help to calm your mind and provide a sense of peace. This can be especially helpful in reducing feelings of anxiety and stress.

Engage in physical activity - Exercise is a great way to cope with stress and manage feelings of anxiety. Whether it's yoga, running, or simply going for a walk, moving your body is an important part of a self-care routine.

Create something - Engaging in creative activities, such as painting, drawing, or writing, can help to provide a sense of accomplishment, release feelings of anger and frustration, and provide a sense of purpose.

_____

_____

_____

CHAPTER 24: STRATEGIES FOR COPING WITH THE AFTERMATH OF VERBAL ABUSE

We are all wounded creatures, struggling to make sense of the hurt and pain that life so often brings us. And when it comes to verbal abuse, the wounds run deep, cutting through our very souls and leaving us feeling lost, broken, and alone.

But in the midst of all this pain, there is hope. There are strategies we can use to help us cope with the aftermath of verbal abuse and begin the process of healing. These strategies are not a panacea, but they can offer us comfort, support, and the chance to reclaim our power and our lives.

The first strategy is to seek out support. Whether it be through therapy, support groups, or close friends and family, it is essential to have people in our lives who understand what we are going through and can offer us love, encouragement, and a shoulder to lean on.

The second strategy is to engage in self-care practices. This can be anything from taking a warm bath, practicing mindfulness, or engaging in physical activity. The important thing is to find what works for us and to make self-care a regular part of our routine.

Finally, it is important to let go of the pain and hurt that we have experienced. This does not mean forgetting or ignoring what has happened to us, but rather accepting it and moving forward with compassion and forgiveness. This can be a difficult and challenging process, but it is essential to our healing and our ability to reclaim our power and our lives.

In the end, healing from the aftermath of verbal abuse is not an easy journey. It requires time, effort, and dedication, but the reward is a life filled with love, hope, and peace. So let us take up this journey with courage and determination, knowing that we are not alone, and that with every step we take, we are one step closer to reclaiming our power and our lives.

Journal Exercises

Create a mind map of all the coping strategies you've tried in the past, both effective and ineffective. Then, consider which strategies you'd like to try in the future and why.

_____

_____

_____

_____

_____

_____

_____

_____

_____

_____

_____

Write a letter to yourself as if you're in the future, reflecting on how far you've come in your healing journey and offering encouragement and advice to your present self.

_____

_____

_____

_____

_____

_____

_____

_____

_____

Imagine yourself standing in front of a mirror. Close your eyes and repeat the following affirmation to yourself three times: "I am worthy and deserving of love, happiness, and healing." Open your eyes and reflect on how you feel.

Write down all the things you're grateful for in your life, no matter how small or seemingly insignificant. Reflect on why you're thankful for each one and how it contributes to your overall well-being.

_____

_____

_____

_____

_____

_____

_____

_____

_____

_____

Make a list of all the people, places, and things that bring you comfort. Then, plan an intentional self-care day around them.

_____

_____

_____

_____

_____

_____

_____

_____

_____

Write a letter to your past self, forgiving them for any mistakes they made and offering them words of encouragement.

Reflect on a time when you stood up for yourself or spoke up about something that mattered to you. Write about the experience, including how you felt and what you learned from it.

Imagine yourself in a peaceful, calming place. Close your eyes and take deep breaths, imagining all the stress and negativity leaving your body. Write about the experience and how you feel.

Write down five goals you have for yourself and why they're important to you. Reflect on how they contribute to your overall well-being and happiness.

Create a self-care plan that includes specific activities, times, and dates to make sure you're taking care of yourself in a consistent and intentional way.

CONCLUSION

Summarizing the Key Points of the Book

Throughout this journey, we've covered the impact of verbal abuse, the process of recognizing and healing from it, and the steps to reclaiming your power and finding your voice. We've explored the role of therapy and support in the healing process, coping strategies for the aftermath of abuse, and the importance of self-love, compassion, and forgiveness in moving forward.

Encouragement to Continue the Journey of Healing and Finding Your Voice

The journey towards healing and finding your voice is not an easy one, but it is a journey worth taking. It takes courage to confront the pain and hurt of past experiences and the strength to reclaim your power and find your voice. It takes patience, perseverance, and self-compassion to navigate the ups and downs of the healing process.

But with every step you take, you are becoming more resilient, more confident, and more empowered. You are reclaiming your life, your identity, and your voice. You are becoming the person you were always meant to be. So, keep moving forward, keep growing, and keep shining.

Final Thoughts and Reflections

As you close this book, take a moment to reflect on your journey so far. Think about the progress you've made, the lessons you've learned, and the person you're becoming.

Recognize your strengths, your courage, and your resilience. Embrace your unique journey and celebrate your progress.

Remember, healing is a lifelong journey, and there will be times when you need to reach out for support, when you need to take a step back and care for yourself, and when you need to embrace self-compassion. But always remember that you are not alone, and you are capable of healing and finding your voice.

With that, I want to thank you for embarking on this journey with me and for the courage you have shown in taking the first steps towards healing and finding your voice. I hope this book has provided you with the support, guidance, and empowerment you need to continue your journey and reach your full potential.

Sincerely,

M.L.Ruscsak

Final thoughts and reflections

Summarizing the Key Points of the Book

Throughout this journey, we've covered the impact of verbal abuse, the process of recognizing and healing from it, and the steps to reclaiming your power and finding your voice. We've explored the role of therapy and support in the healing process, coping strategies for the aftermath of abuse, and the importance of self-love, compassion, and forgiveness in moving forward.

Encouragement to Continue the Journey of Healing and Finding Your Voice

The journey towards healing and finding your voice is not an easy one, but it is a journey worth taking. It takes courage to confront the pain and hurt of past experiences and the strength to reclaim your power and find your voice. It takes patience, perseverance, and self-compassion to navigate the ups and downs of the healing process.

But with every step you take, you are becoming more resilient, more confident, and more empowered. You are reclaiming your life, your identity, and your voice. You are becoming the person you were always meant to be. So, keep moving forward, keep growing, and keep shining.

Final Thoughts and Reflections

As you close this book, take a moment to reflect on your journey so far. Think about the progress you've made, the lessons you've learned, and the person you're becoming. Recognize your strengths, your courage, and your resilience. Embrace your unique journey and celebrate your progress.

Remember, healing is a lifelong journey, and there will be times when you need to reach out for support, when you need to take a step back and care for yourself, and when you need to embrace self-compassion. But always remember that you are not alone, and you are capable of healing and finding your voice.

With that, I want to thank you for embarking on this journey with me and for the courage you have shown in taking the first steps towards healing and finding your voice. I hope this book has provided you with the support, guidance, and empowerment you need to continue your journey and reach your full potential.

Sincerely,
M.L.Ruscsak

Additional Resources
List of books, organizations, and resources for further support and information

Books:

"The Verbally Abusive Relationship" by Patricia Evans
"Why Does He Do That?: Inside the Minds of Angry and Controlling Men" by Lundy Bancroft
"I Know Why the Caged Bird Sings" by Maya Angelou
"The Healing Power of Emotion" by Diana Fosha
"The Body Keeps the Score: Brain, Mind, and Body in the Healing of Trauma" by Bessel van der Kolk
Organizations:

National Domestic Violence Hotline (www.thehotline.org)

National Alliance on Mental Illness (www.nami.org)

Mental Health America (www.mentalhealthamerica.net)

RAINN (Rape, Abuse & Incest National Network) (www.rainn.org)

American Psychological Association (www.apa.org)

Resources for Further Information:

The National Center for Victims of Crime (www.victimsofcrime.org)

The National Resource Center on Domestic Violence (www.nrcdv.org)

The National Verbal Abuse Help Line (www.verbalabuse.com)

The Domestic Abuse Intervention Programs (www.duluth-model.org)

The American Association of Marriage and Family Therapy (www.aamft.org)

www.ingramcontent.com/pod-product-compliance
Lightning Source LLC
Chambersburg PA
CBHW051616120626
46551CB00014B/1815